Upside Down French Toast

Preheat oven to 400
Melt 2 T butter in 9" pan. Into the butter stir 1/4 C brown sugar + 1/4 C crushed pineapple drained of almost all syrup. Spread this mixture evenly over pan.
In bowl beat together 1 egg, 3/4 C milk, 1/8 t salt. Soak 4 slices bread in it until soft then lay over pineapple mixture.

Bake 25 min or until lightly browned & Cool 1 min before inverting on heated platter

THE
Entertaining Woman's
COOKBOOK

THE
Entertaining
Woman's
COOKBOOK

Louise Montague Athearn

ABELARD-SCHUMAN

NEW YORK LONDON

Library of Congress Cataloging in Publication Data

Athearn, Louise, 1931–
   The entertaining woman's cookbook.

   1. Entertaining.   2. Menus.   I. Title.
TX731.A78   641.5   76–157987
ISBN 0–200–71839–8

    NEW YORK   LONDON
  Abelard-Schuman   Abelard-Schuman
      Limited   Limited
257 Park Avenue So.   8 King St. WC2

An Intext Publisher

Printed in the United States of America

Contents

Introduction

Cooking, like lovemaking, is an art. And just as the whole realm of lovemaking is not limited to the boudoir, cooking should not begin and end in the kitchen.

Intrigue should abound in the kitchen as well as in the bedroom. A clever woman knows that a warm oven and a warm bed go hand in glove. Food is sexy and make no mistake about it. Eating and drinking, done properly, touch all the senses all the time. Truly fulfilling the needs of the man in your life is a test of your imagination, intelligence, ingenuity and seductive powers.

This is the book that takes you out of the category of cook and makes you one of the fascinators of the world. Nearly every occasion, real or imagined, is covered. Don't disregard the chapters on hunting or skiing because your husband's interests don't center around these activities. This is a menu cookbook. Every chapter is a treasury of great recipes, all man-tested. With each menu that would be enhanced by wine, you'll find several choices, carefully selected.

As the serving of wine and liquor should be left to the men, I asked a very special man to do the selecting. He's a self-taught authority on wine, a gourmet of the first order, and an appreciator of women—especially of women who are good cooks.

THE
Entertaining Woman's
COOKBOOK

I

Breakfasts and Brunches

Weekend breakfast should feature a good sound cup of coffee or tea, forethought, careful execution—and you! Lovingly. With a smile . . . and in a decent housecoat.

Breakfast for Four Golfers

SCREWDRIVERS
GRAPEFRUIT WITH HONEY
TOTAL OMELETTE
TOAST AND JAM
COFFEE OR TEA

Screwdrivers

For each drink use 2 parts vodka or gin to 4 parts orange juice.* Mix juice and liquor and pour into tall glasses over lots of crushed ice.

Grapefruit with Honey   (Serves 4)

2 grapefruit   8 tablespoons honey

The night before, half the grapefruit and carefully cut around each section. Dribble honey over the entire top. The next morning, broil for about 7 to 10 minutes, until the honey bubbles.

* Frozen orange juice, if prepared in an electric blender, is absolutely delicious, almost as good as hand-squeezed.

Total Omelette   (Serves 4)

¼ to ½ pound Tillamook or
other sharp Cheddar cheese
½ stick butter (⅛ pound)
1 green pepper, chopped
4 or 5 green onions, chopped,
including tops

8 or 10 fresh mushrooms, sliced
2 or 3 tomatoes, chopped, with
skins, seeds and all
2 tablespoons butter
8 eggs
4 tablespoons water

¼ cup chopped parsley

Grate the cheese into a bowl. In an iron skillet melt the ½ stick butter and add the green pepper, onions and mushrooms. Cook until vegetables are soft and mushrooms light brown. Add chopped tomatoes, and let the whole thing simmer on low heat while you do the eggs.

In another iron skillet, melt the 2 tablespoons of butter. Beat the eggs with a wire whisk and add the water. Pour half the eggs into the skillet and, as they cook, push the edges back gently and tip the pan so all the runny part cooks.

When the eggs are almost set, put half the grated cheese on top of the omelette and fold it over. Cut the omelette in half, cook for another minute, and put each half on a warm plate. Spoon the tomato sauce over each serving and sprinkle parsley on top. Serve immediately or keep warm in oven while you repeat the same process with the rest of the eggs.

Breakfast for Four VIP Houseguests

BULLSHOTS
CRÊPES SUZETTE
CANADIAN BACON
PLATTER OF FRESH SLICED PINEAPPLE
COFFEE OR TEA

Bullshot   (Serves 4)

8 jiggers vodka or gin
2 cans consommé or beef bouillon
(or Bullshot Mix)

Worcestershire Sauce
Salt
Pepper

1 lime

In each double Old Fashioned glasses, put ice, 2 jiggers vodka or gin, and fill with consommé. Season with Worcestershire sauce, salt, pepper and a squeeze of lime. Stir well. If you have stoneware mugs, use them. (Steero Company puts out an excellent canned Bullshot Mix to which you just add liquor.)

Crêpes Suzette   (Serves 4)

These are a project. But as with most things in life, once you've done them, they get easier. Make the batter ahead of time and have it ready. Then make the sauce and push it to the back of the stove. You can make crêpes an hour ahead if you like, put them in a tea towel on a cookie sheet and keep warm in the oven. Then, when ready, simply put them in the chafing dish on the buffet, pour the hot sauce over, and stand back!

Crêpes

2 cups flour	1 tablespoon sugar
2 eggs	1 teaspoon salt
2½ cups milk	1 teaspoon vanilla

1 teaspoon butter

Mix flour, eggs, 1½ cups milk, sugar, salt and vanilla. Beat with an egg beater until smooth. Add remaining cup of milk. Beat again. Heat a 6-inch skillet and brush lightly with a little butter. Put in ¾ tablespoon batter; tilt the skillet from side to side so that batter covers the pan. Remember, these are thin crêpes, not pancakes. Brown lightly on each side, fold in half and then in quarters. Put on the cookie sheet, cover with tea towel and keep warm.

Sauce

½ cup butter	2 end slices orange with rind
⅔ cup sugar	1 cup orange juice
1 end slice lemon with rind	1 tablespoon grated orange rind

¼ cup brandy

Grate rind before you cut the orange. In saucepan, heat butter and sugar until it begins to color slightly. Add the lemon and orange end slices, skin side down. Press with the back of a wooden spoon to get out all the good oil. Add orange juice and grated rind. When sauce has bubbled, remove lemon and orange pieces.

To serve, put the crêpes in the chafing dish, pour the sauce over them, and then add the brandy. Light and let flame for a minute or two. These also make a yummy dessert after a light meal. When making the sauce for dessert, add three tablespoons Benedictine and three tablespoons Cointreau in addition to brandy. Deeeeeelicious!

After-tennis Breakfast

SALTY DOGS
PUFFED TOAST
CRISP BACON
COFFEE OR TEA

Salty Dogs   (1 serving)

Take a tall glass, wet the rim, and dip in salt. Fill with ice cubes, add two jiggers vodka or gin and fill up with grapefruit juice. There has never been a better after-tennis drink in the world. Good also after any sport that leaves you heated and panting.

Puffed Toast   (Serves 4)

6 slices bread, ¾ inch thick
8 eggs, beaten slightly
2 cups half-and-half cream
Grated orange rind

½ teaspoon salt
Salad oil
Confectioners' sugar
Maple syrup

Preheat oven to 400°. You need unsliced, day-old bread for this. In fact, two- or three-day-old bread is even better. Cut slices ¾ inch thick and trim off crusts. Cut in half diagonally to form 12 triangles. Combine the eggs, half-and-half, orange rind and salt. Dip bread slices into this mixture and let absorb as much of it as possible.

Fry in ½ inch hot oil in iron skillet. When brown on one side, turn and brown other side. Turn only once. Place slices on a cookie sheet and put them in oven for 3 to 5 minutes. They'll puff up. Drain on paper towel, dust with confectioners' sugar. Serve immediately with syrup. Or serve applesauce, cinnamon or honey.

Brunch in front of a midmorning fire on a gray day, followed by a gin-rummy tournament, is a lovely way to spend the morning.

Fireside Brunch for Six

MILK PUNCH
GRAPEFRUIT MADEIRA
EGGS FLORENTINE
TOASTED ENGLISH MUFFINS
COFFEE OR TEA

Milk Punch   (1 serving)

1 glass milk   1 teaspoon powdered sugar
1½ jiggers brandy

Put in blender with cracked ice and serve in a tall glass.

Grapefruit Madeira   (Serves 6)

3 grapefruit, cut in half   6 to 8 teaspoons brown sugar
6 tablespoons Madeira or sherry

Cut around each section of grapefruit so it will be easy to remove. Sprinkle with brown sugar and broil. Pour a tablespoon of wine over each half just before serving.

Eggs Florentine   (Serves 6)

12 eggs   1 box frozen chopped spinach or
2 bunches fresh, cooked and chopped.

Before you poach the eggs, cook the spinach and line the bottoms of six individual heat-proof dishes. Next, make the sauce.

Sauce

6 tablespoons butter
½ small onion, minced
6 tablespoons flour
2 cups hot milk
½ cup grated Parmesan or Gruyère cheese
1 teaspoon chopped parsley
Salt and pepper to taste

Nutmeg
2 egg yolks
⅓ cup cream
2 tablespoons whipped cream (or fake it with the cream that comes in a pressurized can— but it's only second best.)

Melt butter in a saucepan, add the minced onion and cook until tender. Stir in flour with wire whisk. Keep stirring and gradually add hot milk. Add grated cheese and parsley. Season with salt, pepper and few grains of nutmeg. Keep cooking and stirring until sauce is smooth.

Beat two egg yolks with ⅓ cup cream. Add this and keep stirring until sauce thickens, but don't let it boil. Quickly stir in whipped cream. This is what makes the sauce brown so nicely under the broiler.

Poach 12 eggs and put two into each spinach-lined dish. Cover with the sauce, sprinkle with grated cheese and brown under the broiler. Serve in the dish.

Before-a-Football-game Brunch for Twelve

CHAMPAGNE
GLAZED APPLES
CHEESE SOURDOUGH BAKE
COFFEE OR TEA

CHAMPAGNE:

Laurent Perrier, Brut, N.V. (French)
    or
André, Pink Champagne (California)

Start serving as soon as first guests arrive.

Glazed Apples   (Serves 12)

12 medium-size apples
1¼ cups marmalade
1 cup sugar

6 tablespoons brown sugar
1 cup water
4 tablespoons butter

Cinnamon or nutmeg

Core apples and peel ⅓ way down. Stuff centers with marmalade. Place apples in a small roaster or covered pan. Mix sugars and water together, pour around apples. Top with butter and cinnamon. Cover and bake for 30 minutes in 375° F. oven.

Cheese Sourdough Bake   (Serves 12)

12 slices sourdough French
    bread, buttered and cubed

1½ pounds sharp Cheddar cheese,
    grated

4 green onions, chopped, including green tops

In a greased casserole put alternate layers of bread, cheese, and onions. Place all other ingredients except milk in blender:

9 eggs	¾ teaspoon Lawry's seasoning
1½ teaspoons brown sugar	¾ teaspoon dry mustard
¼ teaspoon paprika	1 tablespoon Worchestershire
¾ teaspoon salt	¼ teaspoon pepper

3¾ cups milk

After this is well blended, add 1¾ cups of the milk and blend again. Pour ½ of this mixture over cheese and bread.

Add 2 cups milk to mixture remaining in blender and blend again. Pour into casserole. Refrigerate overnight.

Remove one hour before baking. Place in cold oven and bake for 1½ hours at 325° F.

Breakfast and brunch can also be exotic. Try this in your garden next spring.

Mexican Breakfast for Eight

CHAMPAGNE WITH PEACH
AVOCADO WITH SOUR CREAM AND CAVIAR
EGGS WITH CHORIZO
CERVEZA MEXICANA BEER
HARD ROLLS WITH BUTTER
COFFEE OR TEA

CHAMPAGNE:

Almadén Blanc de Blancs (California)

or

André (California)

or

Hanns Kornell, Brut (California)

Champagne with Peach

The first course, served to guests on arrival. Peel and halve fresh peaches, allowing one-half peach for each guest. Place peach half in a long-stemmed champagne glass. Fill to top with icy champagne, and serve, giving each guest a spoon.

Seat guests in garden and serve this course while you fix the eggs.

Avocado with Sour Cream and Caviar

4 avocados   Large carton sour cream
                   As much caviar as you can afford

Halve the avocados, but do not peel. Remove seeds, fill each cavity
with sour cream and top with caviar. Don't mix the cream and caviar.
Best to use the caviar unadulterated, even if it's just a teaspoonful.

Eggs with Chorizo   (Serves 8)

4 chorizo sausages   4 to 6 green onions, chopped,
16 eggs   including tops

Chorizos are spicy Mexican sausages, readily available in the delicatessen section of most supermarkets and at specialty markets. The
meat is encased in a fine skin; squeeze it out or peel off the skin. Allow
one-half chorizo for every person. Place an iron skillet on a medium
fire and add the chorizo. With a spatula, break up the pieces as the
meat cooks. Add chopped green onions and mix. In a bowl, break two
eggs per person and beat with a fork. When the chorizo has thoroughly
cooked (about 20 minutes) and looks like a well-done spaghetti sauce,
dump in the eggs. (Chorizo is greasy and you may want to pour off
some of the fat before adding the eggs.) Finish cooking as you would
scrambled eggs. Serve the Mexican beer with the eggs, or just serve
more champagne.

His Birthday Breakfast . . . for Two

     GIN FIZZES
CASABA MELON
EGGS BENEDICT
COFFEE OR TEA

Gin Fizz   (2-plus servings)

4 jiggers gin   ½ teaspoon vanilla
3 egg whites   2 or 3 dashes of orange-flower
½ cup cream   water
2 tablespoons granulated sugar   Juice of 1 lemon
                   1 cup crushed ice

This is not an orthodox recipe; it's my version of an old standby.

Put everything into a blender and blend until frothy. Serve in stemmed wineglasses that have been chilled in the freezer. (Why not wear your velvet culottes?)

Eggs Benedict   (Serves 2)

Make sauce first and keep warm while you poach the eggs.

Hollandaise Sauce

2 egg yolks (left over from fizzes)
1 tablespoon lemon juice

¼ pound butter cut into three pieces
¼ teaspoon salt
Dash cayenne

Put ¾ inch water in bottom of double boiler. Water should simmer but not boil. In top put the egg yolks, lemon juice, and one piece of the butter, softened. Stir constantly. As butter melts, add the second piece and then the third piece. Add salt and cayenne. Keep stirring until thick. If sauce separates, add boiling water a drop at a time.

ALTERNATE: Blender Hollandaise   (very easy)

2 egg yolks
Juice of ½ lemon

½ stick butter (¼ pound)
Worcestershire sauce

Put yolks into blender. Add lemon juice. Melt butter. Turn on blender and slowly add warm butter to yolks. Mix until thickened. Watch carefully, it does not take long. Add dash Worcestershire Sauce.

Eggs, Bacon and Muffins

4 eggs
Butter

4 pieces Canadian bacon
2 English muffins

Butter cups of egg poacher. Put inch of hot water into bottom of pan. Break an egg into each cup, cover, cook over medium heat until whites set. Then fry Canadian bacon, split and toast English muffins.

To assemble, put a piece of bacon on each muffin, then top with a poached egg. Cover the whole thing with hollandaise. As for the traditional slice of truffle on top? Forget it. Tradition is fine if it's inexpensive, which truffles aren't.

Breakfast on the Road

If, for some terribly important reason, you and your husband have to leave home at 4 or 5 Ay-Em to reach a destination by a certain time —say an out-of-town football game—pack a basket and put it in the car the night before. Basket could contain:

    Fruit: grapes, oranges, tangerines or bananas

    Hard rolls

    Plastic dishes of butter and jelly

    Thermos of very hot coffee and two pottery mugs.

    Large napkins

    Package of Wet-Wipes

The only time you should use paper cups for coffee is when it's a choice between that or cupped hands.

II

Outside Eating with Sports

If you have a square of garden, predictable sunshine and a man who loves to do things athletic, plan a "Fat Man's Decathlon." Decide on how many people you are going to invite. Then arrange as many intramural sporting events as space and equipment permit. If you have a swimming pool, a tennis or badminton court, start with relays, water polo and/or mixed doubles. If not, it doesn't matter because there are plenty of other things to set up. Choose as many as you can from the following list:

Croquet, ping-pong, darts, basketball throwing, horseshoes, beanbag toss, races, broad jump, and any others you may wish to add.

Lunch for Sixteen Sports

PLATTER OF RAW VEGETABLES WITH DIPS
PLATTER OF SANDWICH MAKINGS WITH HERB MAYONAISE
BASKETS OF SLICED DARK AND LIGHT BREADS
ALLIANCE ASPIC
BEAN SALAD
COLD BEER
PLATTER OF COOKIES
COFFEE

Raw Vegetables

Cauliflower   Turnips
Celery sticks   Cucumber sticks
Carrot curls   Watercress
Green onions   Radishes
              Cherry tomatoes

In the morning wash and cut the vegetables into sizes and shapes that are suitable for picking up in the fingers. Store in foil in refrigerator. To serve, arrange on platter with dips in the middle.

Anchovy Dip

4 2-ounce cans anchovy fillets   1 clove garlic, crushed
1 tablespoon butter   3 tablespoons white wine vinegar
                3 tablespoons salad oil

Wash the fillets to remove oil and salt. Put everything into a saucepan and heat, stirring constantly until it forms a paste. Put into small bowl for center of platter. Refrigerate until needed.

Cottage Cheese Dip

1 carton cottage cheese   2 tablespoons sour cream
¼ teaspoon garlic salt   Juice of ½ lemon
2 green onions, chopped with   4 to 6 tablespoons pickled herring
   tops   finely chopped

Mix and mash all together or put in blender to mix. Refrigerate until needed.

Herb Mayonnaise   (to serve with cold cuts)

1 cup mayonnaise   ½ cup sour cream
½ tablespoon lemon juice   1 tablespoon grated onion
¼ teaspoon salt   1 clove garlic, minced
¼ teaspoon paprika   1 tablespoon chopped chives
1 teaspoon mixed herbs   ⅛ tablespoon curry powder
          ½ teaspoon Worcestershire sauce

Mix all together and serve in bowl. Save any left over to make delicious sandwich spread or salad dressing for the next day.

Alliance Aspic   (Serves 12 to 16)

1 cup cold Bloody Mary mix
4½ envelopes unflavored gelatin
2 teaspoons Worcestershire
   sauce
4½ cups hot tomato juice
½ teaspoon seasoned salt
½ teaspoon garlic salt
½ teaspoon pepper
3 tablespoons fresh lemon juice

Soften gelatin in cold mix, then dissolve thoroughly in very hot tomato juice. Season and set container in pan of cold water.

FILLING:

12 ounces cream cheese
1 cup sour cream
1½ envelopes unflavored gelatin
   dissolved in ¼ cup cold water

The day before use, blend cream cheese and sour cream in top pan of a double boiler. Place container of softened gelatin in pan of boiling water and when thoroughly dissolved add to cream mixture. Fill bottom pan of double boiler half-full of water and bring to the boiling point. Turn heat low and set the cream cheese mixture in its pan over it to keep soft.

Rub an 8-cup loaf mold with salad oil. When aspic has thickened slightly, put ⅓ of it into mold. Set in freezer to hasten hardening. When aspic is firm, spread on ½ the cream-cheese mixture. Return to freezer. Then add another layer of aspic, then cheese and end with aspic (5 layers). Chill overnight.

To serve, unmold onto platter, cut ¾-inch slices, then cut each slice in half.

Bean Salad   (Serves 16)

2 large cans whole tiny green
   beans
1 large can wax beans
1 large can kidney beans
2 large cans garbanza beans
1 teaspoon salt
½ teaspoon pepper
¾ cup sugar
⅓ cup salad oil
⅔ cup cider vinegar

Drain beans and put into a large bowl. Add rest of ingredients, mix well and refrigerate for 24 hours if possible. Drain liquid before serving.

Around-the-pool Luau for Twelve

MAI TAIS

HIBACHI HORS D'OEUVRES

SEA FOOD GALAXY WITH RICE IN PINEAPPLE BOATS

ORANGE AND GRAPEFRUIT BOWL

CHOCOLATE DIP

KONA KOFFEE

WINE TO SERVE:

Charles Krug, Chenin Blanc (California)
> or

Jadot, Pouilly-Fuissé, (French)
> or

Mirassou, Pinot Blanc (California)
> or

Gallo, Rhine Garten (California)

Mai Tais for 12   (makes 8 quarts.)

2 quarts Bacardi rum	1 quart curaçao
1 quart Jamaica rum	1½ quarts lemon juice
¾ quart Demerara rum	1¼ quarts orange juice

1 pint grenadine

Mix all together, put into tightly covered jars or bottles and store in the refrigerator. It will keep all summer.

To serve, pour over ice cubes in an iced-tea glass, add a piece of pineapple and a cherry or sprig of mint. If it seems too strong, add a shot of soda water. (Of course you can buy Mai Tai mix already made.)

Pineapple Boats

The instructions are given in the order of easiest preparation.

Take two fresh pineapples and halve them vertically, cutting through the leaves. Retain the leaves. With a sharp knife, cut under the pineapple meat and ease it out. Sometimes it helps to cut down through the middle of the meat and take out the core first so as to end up with an empty half-pineapple shell, complete with leaves. Save pineapple meat in a bowl and invert shells on piece of paper towel to drain.

Hibachi Hors d'Oeuvres   (Serves 12)

Cooked over a hibachi. What else?

Take the best-looking pieces of pineapple meat and set aside for the Mai Tais; cut the rest into bite-size pieces. Wrap each piece in bacon and secure by fastening on end of metal spear or barbecue fork. Guests cook them over the hibachi and then dip in sauce.

Buy 2 pounds of the best all-beef hot dogs. Cut into bite-size pieces to be cooked over hibachi and dipped in sauce.

Easy Sauce I

½ cup catsup
1 teaspoon dry mustard
3 dashes Tabasco Sauce

1 tablespoon Worcestershire
sauce

Mix all together. Makes about ½ cup.

Easy Sauce II

½ cup chopped onion
¼ cup butter

1⅓ cups chili sauce
⅓ cup A-1 sauce

Sauté the onion in butter until tender. Add rest of ingredients. Mix all together. Makes 1¾ cups of sauce.

Serving the hors d'oeuvres this way is good for the players. They can cook them as they want them, and get warm at the same time.

Seafood Galaxy with Rice   (Serves 12)

2 4-ounce cans sliced mushrooms, drained
2 tablespoons butter
2 10-ounce cans frozen condensed cream-of-shrimp soup
1 cup light cream

4 to 6 cups cut-up cooked seafood (crab, whitefish, lobster, scallops, shrimp)
½ cup shredded Cheddar cheese or sharp American cheese
6 tablespoons sherry.

Brown mushrooms lightly in butter. Add soup and cream; heat slowly until thawed. Add seafood and cheese ten minutes before serving. Add sherry just before serving. Warm pineapple shells in a moderate oven for about 10 minutes. Fill with the seafood and serve.

RICE: Buy regular long grain packaged rice (not instant) and prepare according to directions.

Serve in a large wooden salad bowl placed next to the pineapple shells. Guests help themselves to rice, then to seafood.

Orange and Grapefruit Bowl   (Serves 12)

8 oranges   4 grapefruit

Peel and cut the individual sections away from the membranes and marinate in this dressing. Prepare in the morning and let chill all day.

Dressing

1 teaspoon dry mustard   1 cup catsup
2 tablespoons sugar   2 cups salad oil
2 teaspoons salt   Juice of four lemons

Put into jar with a tight lid and shake well.

Chocolate Dip   (Serves 6)

24 ounces (2 bars) milk   4 medium-size bananas, cut in
   chocolate or   1-inch chunks
24 ounces semisweet chocolate   1 angel-food cake (or 2 pound
1½ cups whipping cream   cakes) cut into cubes
⅓ cup Cointreau

Place chocolate and cream in the top of a double boiler, set over hot but not boiling water and heat, stirring, until chocolate melts and blends with cream. Stir in Cointreau. Transfer to a small pan (fondue pot is a good one) and place over a candle warmer or electric food warmer. Or use the top pan of a small chafing dish with hot-water under it. Be careful not to overheat chocolate sauce or it may scorch. Place bananas and cake cubes on tray with fondue forks beside the hot chocolate sauce. Spear fruit or cake on fork and swirl in the chocolate. (Everyone visits the chocolate pot to dip, dribble, and drool.)

Kona Koffee

Ground coffee from Hawaii that you make the regular way.

Outside Gourmet Dinner for Six

Be unpredictable! Instead of having a casual patio barbecue, plan a gourmet dinner—complete with crystal, silver, white linen and best china—served outside. And, of course, ask your guests to dress.

MUSHROOMS WITH CAVIAR
STEAK IN BOURBON MARINADE
STUFFED ZUCCHINI
GREEN GODDESS SALAD
PEACH COUPE WITH CHERRIES JUBILEE
COFFEE

BEFORE DINNER:

Serve an aperitif rather than cocktails.

Heitz Cellar, Sherry

or

Gallo, Old Decanter Very Dry Sherry

or

Byrrh, a French aperitif with a slight brandy flavor

TO SERVE WITH DINNER:

Louis Martini, Cabernet Sauvignon (California)

or

Almadén, Cabernet Sauvignon (California)

or

Clos de Vougeot (French)

Mushrooms with Caviar   (Serves 6)

24 to 36 medium to small fresh
   mushroom caps
Bottle of vinegar-and-oil salad
   dressing

½ pint sour cream
1 small jar red caviar
Lemon juice

Clean mushrooms and marinate in the bottled dressing all day if possible. When ready to serve, wipe with dampened paper towel, and arrange on tray. Blend sour cream and caviar. Brush inside of mushrooms with lemon juice. Fill with sour-cream mixture.

Steak in Bourbon Marinade   (Serves 6)

Parsley
2 onions, thinly sliced
1 carrot thinly sliced
2 shallots, minced

12 peppercorns
2 whole cloves
1 cup bourbon
½ cup olive oil

Large thick slice of top sirloin (about 3½-5 pounds)

Mix together all ingredients except steak to make marinade. Marinate steak for at least 3 hours, turning often so that every thirsty fiber can soak up its share of this heady liquid. Broil or barbecue steak. Slice thinly on the diagonal and serve on silver platter with parsley garnish.

Stuffed Zucchini   (Serves 6)

6 medium-size zucchini (Italian
   squash)
3 cups soft bread crumbs
½ cup grated Parmesan cheese
1 small onion, chopped fine

3 tablespoons chopped parsley
1 teaspoon salt
⅛ teaspoon pepper
2 well-beaten eggs
1 stick butter (¼ pound)

Wash the zucchini. Cut off ends, but don't pare. Boil in salted water for 5 minutes. Halve lengthwise. Carefully remove pulp with spoon. Combine pulp with bread crumbs, grated cheese, onion, parsley, salt, pepper and eggs. Fill zucchini shells with mixture, dot with butter and sprinkle with additional cheese. Place in well-oiled (olive oil) shallow pan and bake in 350° F. oven for 30 minutes.

Green Goddess Salad   (Serves 6)

2 heads butter lettuce, washed, dried and broken into pieces.

DRESSING: 1 cup mayonnaise
          1 tablespoon vinegar
          2 teaspoons anchovy
             paste
          2 teaspoons chopped chives

1 handful parsley with stems
   removed
2 tablespoons sour cream
1 teaspoon freshly ground pepper

Put everything into blender and blend dressing until smooth. Serve over the lettuce.

Peach Coupe with Cherries Jubilee   (Serves 6)

1 can (1 pound 14 ounces) pitted
   black cherries
1 tablespoon sugar
1 tablespoon cornstarch
1 cup cherry juice

1 piece (½ inch by 1½ inches)
   lemon peel
2 tablespoons cherry liqueur
⅓ cup brandy, warmed
1 pint vanilla ice cream

6 peach halves (canned or fresh)

Drain cherries and save juice. Mix sugar with cornstarch and add 1 cup cherry juice a little at a time. Add lemon peel and cook gently until mixture is clear and thickened (about 5 minutes). Remove from heat. Take out lemon peel, stir in cherry liqueur and the cherries. This sauce may be prepared ahead of time.

To serve, have the dessert dishes ready on a tray at the table. Place peach halves in deep platter and fill each with scoop of ice cream. Transfer the cherry sauce to a chafing dish and heat gently. Pour the warm brandy over the hot sauce, without stirring. Set ablaze and spoon cherries and sauce over peaches and ice cream. With large spoon lift peaches onto dessert plates.

III

The Fine Art of Tailgating

To a modern hostess, to "tailgate" means to picnic from the rear of a station wagon—or from a Rolls Royce, for that matter. But it's picnicking with Lucullus. It's pâté and chilled champagne, boned breast of chicken and avocado soup, tiny pastries and Grand Marnier.

Tailgating can mean serving two or twenty-two. It involves flatware and hamper, wineglasses and napkins. It requires special containers as the hot must be hot and the cold, cold. It must be planned with care, engineered with precision, and served with ease.

Picnic before a Polo Match—for 4

AVOCADO SOUP
CAULIFLOWER SALAD
RICE AND SHRIMP PILAF
CHEESE STRAWS
PINEAPPLE SURPRISE
COOKIES
HOT COFFEE

WINE TO SERVE:

Christian Brothers, Sauvignon Blanc (California)
 or
Gallo, Pink Chablis (California)
 or
Italian Swiss Colony, Rhineskeller (California)

Avocado Soup   (Serves 2)

2 ripe avocados, peeled and pitted
4 cups canned chicken broth (or
use chicken-bouillon cubes, 8
cubes to 4 cups of hot water)
2 cups cream

4 tablespoons rum (light)
1 teaspoon curry powder
1 teaspoon seasoned salt
Freshly ground pepper (put small
mill in hamper)

1 lemon, quartered

Put everything but lemon into blender. Mix and chill. Pour into thermos. Serve in mugs with lemon on the side. Guests grind a bit of pepper on top.

Cauliflower Salad   (Serves 4)

1 small head cauliflower
4 slices of bacon
¼ cup salad oil

¼ cup vinegar
1½ teaspoons salt
1 teaspoon sugar

¼ teaspoon paprika

Trim the cauliflower, take out and discard the hard core and slice remainder crosswise very thinly. Put into a bowl. Fry bacon very crisp, drain and crumble it over cauliflower. Add rest of ingredients to bacon grease in pan, stir and pour over cauliflower. Refrigerate for at least 3 hours. Put salad in plastic bag and put in picnic ice chest.

Rice and Shrimp Pilaf   (Serves 4)

1 package frozen shrimp
1 cup quick-cooking brown rice
1½ cups boiling water
2 chicken bouillon cubes

6 tablespoons mayonnaise
½ cup oil and vinegar dressing
(bottled is fine)
½ teaspoon thyme

1 teaspoon curry powder

Add the rice and the bouillon cubes to the boiling water. Reduce heat, cover pan, and steam for 15 minutes. Chill. Make dressing of the rest of the ingredients. Cook shrimp according to directions on package and add with dressing to rice. Toss well and rechill. Pack in bowl covered with foil and place in ice chest. Serve on plate with the cauliflower salad.

Cheese Straws

Buy in a package. Why fight it?

Pineapple Surprise   (Serves 4)

1 small ripe pineapple
1 cup dry white wine or 1 cup
   Triple Sec

1 box fresh strawberries
Sprigs of fresh mint

Pare and slice the pineapple into bite-size pieces discarding pulpy core. Marinate in white wine for several hours in refrigerator. Divide pineapple and marinade into four servings and put into paper or plastic cups with lids. Decorate with strawberries and fresh mint. Put lid on tight. Store in ice chest.

COOKIES: Buy at bakery and keep in the bakery box.

Infield Party for Twenty-Four

One of the most original tailgatings I've ever witnessed was an In-field Party after the last race at Santa Anita Race Track in Arcadia, California . . . given by two bachelors!

COCKTAILS
CHIPS AND DIPS
4 BUTTERFLIED LEGS OF LAMB
BAKED MUSHROOMS AND LIMA BEANS
MIXED SALAD
KEG OF BEER
FRENCH BREAD WITH HERBS
COFFEE BROWNIES
COFFEE

COCKTAILS:

Turn this over to HIM.

Hors d'Oeuvres

Everyone will want to nibble on something, but don't offer too much. (Remember, everyone had a big lunch at the clubhouse dining room.) Potato chips and dips are a good choice. Buy six bags of chips in assorted flavors: barbecue, onion, cheese, corn.

Blue Cheese and Sherry Dip

4 4-ounce packages blue cheese   2 2-ounce packages cream cheese
                            Sherry

Combine cheeses in bowl. Soften with sherry until of dip consistency.
Cover bowl with Saran wrap. Do not refrigerate. The longer it has to
wait to be eaten the better it is, within reason, of course.

Minced Clam Dip

1 8-ounce can minced clams   1 tablespoon Worcestershire
1 8-ounce package cream cheese   sauce
¼ cup sherry   ½ teaspoon paprika

Drain clams and save juice. Keep cheese at room temperature until
soft, then thin with clam juice and sherry. Add clams, Worcestershire
sauce and paprika. Mix well and chill. This must be kept in ice chest.

Butterflied Legs of Lamb   (Serves 24)

The day before the party have your favorite butcher bone four legs
of lamb. Marinate overnight in your refrigerator. (Spread out, the meat
looks like a "butterfly.")

Marinade for Lamb   (Divide in four for one leg of lamb.)

4 small jars mint jelly   4 jars salad oil, mix half olive and
                            half vegetable oil (Use an empty
                            mint jelly jar for measure.)
                  4 tablespoons garlic salt

Melt the jelly in a pan over low fire. Add the oil and salt. Put each
leg (or two together) into a heavy plastic bag. Pour in marinade and tie
end of bag securely. Refrigerate overnight. Turn bag over a couple of
times if you're up late.

The next day the lamb, in the bags of marinade, may stay out of
ice chest in a cool spot until barbecue time. You might put a couple of
layers of foil around them.

When ready, build a good fire in your portable barbecue as you would for steaks. As you turn the lamb on the grill, dribble marinade over the top. Remember: Bring a large wooden platter to carve on, a sharp knife and a long handled fork.

Baked Mushrooms and Lima Beans
(2 casseroles, serve 12 each)

1 pound fresh mushrooms
8 onions, chopped
8 tablespoons butter
2 cans cream of mushroom soup
2 tablespoons Worcestershire
  sauce

1 teaspoon salt
1 teaspoon pepper
6 packages frozen baby lima beans
1 cup Parmesan cheese
1 cup heavy cream

Slice the mushrooms. In a big frying pan, sauté the onions and mushrooms in butter until limp. Stir in the soup and seasonings. Cook the beans according to directions but only about 5 minutes. Combine with onions and mushrooms and turn into two large greased casseroles. Mix cheese and cream and pour half over the top of each casserole. Bake 30 to 35 minutes in 350° F. oven.

Cover and wrap well in newspaper to keep warm. Reheat on barbecue if necessary. (Quarter the amounts to make a terrific casserole for 6.)

Mixed Green Salad   (Serves 24)

4 plastic bags of salad greens—
  spinach, red lettuce, head
  lettuce, romaine, watercress—
  any kind fresh.
8 tomatoes, sectioned

4 avocados
2 bunches green onions, chopped
  with tops. (Store in separate
  plastic bag.)

Just before dinner assemble all ingredients in four wooden bowls. Don't forget to take a large fork and spoon to toss the salad, a sharp knife to cut the avocados.

Salad Dressing for Mixed Greens

½ cup catsup
½ cup salad oil
1 tablespoon brown sugar
2 tablespoons vinegar
1½ tablespoons prepared mustard

1½ tablespoons Worcestershire
  sauce
½ teaspoon seasoned salt
1 clove garlic, minced
½ a medium orange, unpeeled,
  cut in paper-thin slices

Combine all ingredients except orange in quart jar. Cover and shake well. Add orange slices, cover and chill overnight. Makes about two cups. Transport to picnic in container with a tight lid.

French Bread with Herbs   (Serves 24)

Slice 4 loaves of French bread just to—but not through—the under crust. Spread with soft butter mixed with crushed garlic, oregano and paprika. Wrap in foil. Heat on barbecue while you carve the lamb.

Coffee Brownies   (Makes 16 pieces)

¾ cup flour
½ teaspoon baking powder
¼ teaspoon salt
2 tablespoons instant coffee
2 squares unsweetened chocolate

⅓ cup butter
2 eggs, unbeaten
1 cup granulated sugar
1 teaspoon vanilla
½ cup chopped walnuts

(Double or triple recipe quantities if more are wanted.)

Sift together flour, baking powder, salt and coffee. Melt chocolate with butter in top of double boiler over hot water. Cool. Beat eggs with sugar and add to chocolate. Stir flour mixture into chocolate. Add vanilla and nuts and mix thoroughly. Pour into greased 8″ × 8″ × 2″ pan and bake for 25 minutes in 375° F. oven.

COFFEE: Take along a 30-cup electric percolator. Remember to check whether there is electricity available and whether you'll need extension cords. Also, take sugar cubes and a cream substitute or canned milk.

A lovely way to entertain during the summer months is to plan a dinner that you can eat at an open-air concert—at the Hollywood Bowl in California, for instance.

Concert Dinner for Four

PÂTÉ, BLACK BREAD WITH SWEET BUTTER
COLD ARTICHOKES AND DIP
CHICKEN BREASTS IN SOUR CREAM
SPICED PEARS
COFFEE
SWEETS

WINE TO SERVE:

Dom Perignon, Champagne (French)
    or
Mirassou Natural Champagne (California)
    or
André, Champagne (California)

WINE TO USE FOR PEARS:

Charles Krug, Pinot Noir (California)

or

Louis Martini, Cabernet Sauvignon (California)

THE WINE: All the experts chose champagne and champagne must be cold—icy cold. Be sure it's well chilled during the day. If it's a long ride to the theater or park, keep it on ice in a bucket. Take *real* champagne glasses. They don't have to be your best crystal, but they should be glass.

PÂTÉ: Buy a really good tinned pâté or prepare:

Mock Foie Gras

1 pound chicken livers	2 tablespoons mayonnaise
½ tablespoon chow-chow pickles	¼ cup finely chopped celery
¼ teaspoon Tabasco	¼ an onion, grated
¼ teaspoon Worcestershire sauce	Salt and pepper to taste

Broil livers in butter and put through food chopper or grinder. Mix with rest of ingredients and form into two mounds on a plate. Chill.

Take one with you and have the other next week on a picnic in the woods with a cold split and a warm beau.

Black Bread

Buy a loaf of unsliced black bread. Freeze and, while frozen, slice as thin as possible. An electric knife works wonders with frozen bread. Let bread thaw, spread with butter and wrap in foil. Canned pumpernickel rounds can also be used. You will find them in the gourmet section of most supermarkets.

Sweet Butter: Sweet butter is unsalted butter, which most supermarkets carry.

Cold Artichokes

Allow 1 artichoke per person. Wash artichokes in cold water and drain all excess moisture. With a very sharp knife cut off stem flush with the bottom of the artichoke so it has a flat bottom surface to stand on. Pull off the outer woody leaves around the bottom.

On a cutting board, hold the artichoke on its side and cut off the upper third, removing the prickly tips of all the leaves. Or use sharp kitchen scissors and cut each leaf. (This takes longer.) Use a melon-ball scoop or a small spoon to scoop out the center and the fuzzy core. Dip the cut leaf edges in lemon juice to keep from discoloring, if you're a purist.

To cook, place the artichokes, bottom side down, in about one inch of boiling salted water (I use half water and half wine) in a large pan with a lid. Cook, covered, until tender (about 45 minutes). Refrigerate. Just before leaving, fill centers with dip and securely wrap in Saran. Guests remove outer leaves, dip in center till all are eaten.

Horseradish Dip for Cold Artichoke

¼ teaspoon horseradish
½ teaspoon salt

¼ teaspoon freshly ground pepper
1 cup sour cream

Mix altogether and fill chokes. What you have left, put away to use for sandwiches.

Chicken Breasts in Sour Cream   (Serves 4)

3 chicken breasts, boned and cut in half (1 piece for each lady, 2 for each gentleman)
1 small carton sour cream
1 tablespoon lemon juice

1 teaspoon Worcestershire sauce
1 teaspoon seasoned salt
½ teaspoon seasoned pepper
½ teaspoon paprika
½ box garlic croutons

Mix the sour cream with all the seasonings. Coat each piece of chicken heavily and put into Pyrex baking pan. (Yes, you do have to use your hands. There is no other way.) Put the croutons between two pieces of wax paper and crush with rolling pin. Sprinkle over chicken. Bake at 350° F. for 45 minutes.

Good hot or cold. Don't substitute plain crumbs for the croutons—it just isn't the same!

NOTE: You can also make garlic crumbs by rubbing cold toast with a peeled clove of garlic and putting it into the blender. The harder the toast, the better it crumbles.

Spiced Pears   (Serves 4)

4 large pears
1 cup red wine (claret or burgundy are fine)

3 tablespoons granulated sugar
1 stick cinnamon
Small piece lemon rind

Peel the pears, halve, and core. In skillet combine wine, sugar, cinnamon and lemon rind and bring to boil. Add pears and cover. Simmer for about 40 minutes or until pears are tender, turning once. Put each pear and some syrup into individual paper or plastic cups with lids and secure tightly.

COFFEE: Thermos of hot coffee and mugs—*not* paper cups, please.

SWEETS: To munch on during the second half of the program (quietly, of course) take along a sack of good bakery cookies.

Dinner for Eight in the Park before a Concert

GIN 'N TONICS

SHRIMP IN BEER

ASPARAGUS-LEEK SOUP

CHERRY TOMATOES

GREEN OLIVES

GREEN ONIONS

BLACK BREAD AND BUTTER

GRAPES AND CHEESE

COFFEE

TO SERVE:

Cold Danish Beer

Gin 'N' Tonics: Take bottles of gin, small bottles of tonic, fresh limes and plenty of ice. (Pack beer in the ice.)

Shrimp in Beer   (Serves 8)

These have to be cooked at the picnic, so plan for your fire. Some markets and garden-supply stores carry prefabricated little barbecues. They are all-in-one packages, about the size of two shoe boxes. They contain the briquettes, lighter fluid, and the grille. When you're through, you simply douse the fire with water or sand. Take home and dispose of them. If you can't find the packaged barbecues, pick a park that has fireplaces you can use. Take your own small grill (you know its state of cleanliness) charcoal, lighter fluid.

2 pounds unshelled shrimp
1 large onion, sliced thin
2 cloves garlic, crushed
1½ teaspoons salt

1 teaspoon hot pepper sauce
1 green pepper, finely chopped
2 to 3 cups beer
Metal skewers

Split the shrimp down the back with scissors or with a special tool designed for this purpose. Remove the back vein, but leave the shells on. Place in a bowl with the onion, garlic, salt, hot sauce and green pepper. Cover with beer and marinate for 6 to 8 hours or overnight. Pack in plastic bag and keep in ice chest. When fire is ready, spear a shrimp and broil over charcoal fire.

Asparagus-Leek Soup   (Serves 8)

2 packages frozen cut asparagus	½ teaspoon pepper
1½ cups boiling water	Salt to taste
2 envelopes leek soup mix	Sour cream
6 cups milk	Chopped chives

Cook the frozen asparagus in the boiling water until it is tender. Pour the cooked asparagus, including the water, into the blender and whirl until smooth. Add the leek soup mix, 3 cups milk and the pepper. Blend. Pour into a pan, add the rest of the milk and heat. Add salt.

Put soup into large thermos. Serve in pottery mugs with a dollop of sour cream and the chives floating on top. Pass black bread and butter.

One way to endear yourself to a dog-fancying man is to be genuinely interested in his dog or dogs. And there are times, believe it or not, when you can plan a festive outing with dogs. And men, naturally. For instance, Field Trials.

Field Trial Brunch for Four

HOT SPIKED TEA (It's fall or spring and chilly)
PEELED ORANGES
HOT CROSS BUNS OR CINNAMON ROLLS
BAKED APPLE WITH SOUR CREAM
DOG BISCUITS (for the dogs, of course)

Spiked Tea   (Serves 12)

Others at the Trials won't be as clever as you, so why not bring plenty of hot tea? For them, paper cups. For your four, pottery mugs.

1 heaping tablespoon orange
  pekoe tea
1 quart boiling water
6 large lemons

1 pint cold water
1 stick cinnamon
1 cup sugar
2 or 3 cups sherry

Steep tea in boiling water for 15 minutes. Squeeze juice from lemons.

Put juice, lemon skins, cold water and cinnamon stick into a pan and gently simmer until lemon skins are tender. Strain and add the sugar. Strain tea and combine the two. Immediately pour into two thermos jugs. Add sherry just before serving, about 1½ cups to each thermos.

PEELED ORANGES: Simply take along several large oranges that are suitable for peeling, sectioning and eating. Let guests peel their own.

HOT CROSS BUNS OR CINNAMON ROLLS: Buy from your favorite bake shop. Heat and wrap in foil or take in bun warmer.

Baked Apples with Sour Cream   (Serves 4)

4 apples
4 teaspoons drained crushed
  pineapple

4 teaspoons brown sugar
Sour cream
Cinnamon, ground

Core apples, but don't go through bottom. Peel off 1 inch of skin around top. Put teaspoon of pineapple and brown sugar in each center. Place apples, top up, in baking dish with 6 to 8 tablespoons water. Bake in 375° F. oven for 30 minutes or until done. Place each apple on a square of heavy foil. Wrap up securely. Take sour cream in carton and small can of ground cinnamon to dust on it. To eat, peel back the foil, spoon on cream and dig out apple with teaspoon.

IV

On the Beach, at the Lake, in the Mountains

Summer is beach time. And if you own or rent a beach house, middle-of-the-week cooking, when your man's not there, can be as simple or elaborate as you like. But come Friday night, the picture changes. Drastically. On Friday night it's a good idea to plan an expandable dinner. He may get generous at the last minute and invite an extra couple or two for the weekend.

Expandable Friday-night Dinner for Four to Fourteen

BREAKERS CASSEROLE
TOSSED GREEN SALAD
HOT FRENCH ROLLS
FRUIT SHERBET WITH COOKIES
COFFEE

TO SERVE:
Gallo, Paisano (California)
or
Charles Krug, Mt. Zinfandel (California)
or
Villa Antinori, Chianti (Italian)

Don't buy Chianti in raffia-covered bottles unless you are sure of the vintner. Buy, rather, in straight-sided Bordeaux bottles.

Breaker's Casserole   (Serves four—teen)

2 tablespoons olive oil
1 cup chopped onion
¾ cup chopped green pepper
2 cloves garlic, crushed
1 large can tomatoes (at least 13 ounces)
2 pounds ground chuck
2 cups canned whole-kernel corn, drained

¼ cup tomato paste
2 teaspoons salt
1 teaspoon oregano
½ teaspoon seasoned pepper
¼ teaspoon allspice
1¼ cups grated Cheddar cheese
1 cup sliced pitted olives
1 pound fettucini (or about 1 pound for every four people.)

Heat the oil in a large skillet and sauté the onion, green pepper and garlic until tender. Add the ground beef, break it up with a fork and brown well. Add the tomatoes, corn, tomato paste, salt, oregano, pepper and allspice. Simmer slowly for 20 minutes, stirring occasionally. Add the cheese and olives and mix well.

Just before serving, cook the fettucini, drain and serve on platter with the sauce for 4 to 8 people. *To expand*, add: 1 pound meat, 1 cup corn, 1 small can tomato sauce, more chopped green pepper and onions, more cheese and a pinch or two of each seasoning.

Salad

When you come home from the market, put all the greens you've bought for the weekend into cold water. Wash the lettuce but don't separate the leaves from the stems or pull apart the head lettuce. Drain, dry; put into plastic bags and store in refrigerator until ready to use. Break up enough lettuce at serving time to accommodate the crowd and toss with bottled dressing. (I mean, *who* makes salad dressing at the beach?)

It's a good idea to wash all the things used in salads ahead of time, because washing and trying to dry at the last minute is what makes salads watery and the dressing weak. Another thing to do ahead of time is to make croutons in the morning; let it dry out, then rub hard with a peeled clove of garlic. To use, cut up and toss with the salad greens.

FRUIT SHERBET: Allow 1 pint of sherbet for each 4 people.

Saturday Night Beach Barbecue for 6 or 8

SEVEN-BONE BEEF ROAST IN LAGUNA MARINADE

BEACH CORN

TOSSED SALAD

COOKIES

COFFEE

TO SERVE:

Charles Krug, Burgundy (California)

or

Sebastiani, Barbera (California)

or

Italian Swiss Colony, Mt. Zinfandel (California)

Seven-Bone Roast

Buy 4-inches-thick roast. Put in Pyrex pan to marinate as soon as you get home from the store on Friday. Turn whenever you think about it. Drain, wrap in foil and keep cool till barbecue time.

Laguna Marinade

1 cup bourbon   1 cup honey

½ cup soy sauce

Beach Corn

Take unhusked corn (one ear for each woman, two for each man) to the beach with you in the morning cut off tassels and soak in a washtub of ocean water. When you get ready to cook the meat (fire will be gray coals), put corn as is (in husks) on grill surrounding meat. Put the "handle" end of the corn to the outside so you can turn the ears without losing three fingers. Corn husks will turn black on the outside, but that's all right. If it's windy, put a large piece of foil over the corn on the fire.

To serve, melt ½ pound of butter in rectangular Pyrex cake pan, shuck the ears and roll them in it. Don't add any seasoning as something in the ocean water gives the corn an entirely new flavor.

COFFEE: In the morning make a pot of coffee in your 30-cup electric coffee maker and pour into a giant metal coffee pot with a handle. This goes on the grill to heat while dinner is being eaten.

If you have been looking all summer for a large coffee pot, go to a restaurant and hotel supply house. They have great things to use for large crowds. To add one such item a summer is a good investment.

Beach Barbecue for 10 to 12

FRENCH HAMBURGERS

SALAD NIÇOISE

CUPCAKES

COFFEE

TO SERVE:

Inglenook, Pinot Noir (California)
or
Louis Martini, Burgundy (California)
or
Gallo, Hearty Burgundy (California)

French Hamburgers (Serves 10 to 12)

2 round loaves French bread
2 sticks (½ pound) butter, softened
1 teaspoon prepared mustard
1 teaspoon chili powder
6 pounds ground chuck

4 teaspoons seasoned salt
1 cup finely chopped green onions, including tops
4 tablespoons chili sauce
2 tablespoons soy sauce
2 tablespoons A-1 sauce

Cut the loaves of bread in half horizontally. Turn each half over and cut a very tiny slice off crust so bread will sit straight on plate later. Spread the cut surfaces (not bottom) with soft butter mixed with the mustard and chili powder. Combine the ground chuck with salt, onions, chili sauce and other seasonings. Shape into four patties, each a little larger than the bread as the meat shrinks when cooked.

Place the bread, buttered surface down, at the back of the grill to heat slowly. Barbecue the meat patties on one side, then turn over and put bread on top of them. Continue cooking until meat is done. Invert on a plate (bread side down) and cut each half into three or four wedges. A thin slice of tomato may be placed on top of each serving.

Salad Niçoise

2 pounds potatoes, boiled and sliced
2 cans cut green beans, drained
1 can artichoke hearts
1 large onion, thinly sliced
Salad greens
1 box cherry tomatoes
1 cup pitted black olives

6 hard-boiled eggs, quartered
1 large green pepper cut in rings
½ cup canned red-pepper strips
2 2-ounce cans rolled anchovies with capers
¼ cup chopped parsley
Garlic dressing (see below)

For a weekend party, on Friday night or Saturday morning boil, peel and slice the potatoes. Put them into a large bowl with the beans, artichoke hearts and onion. Pour a cup of dressing over them and put in refrigerator.

When ready to serve, line a bowl with greens and spoon the mixed vegetables in with a slotted spoon. Save the dressing.

On top of the dressed vegetables put tomatoes, olives, eggs, peppers and anchovies. Sprinkle with parsley and pass a bowl of reserved dressing. If needed, add more dressing to what is left from the vegetables.

Garlic Dressing

2 cups olive oil
½ cup tarragon vinegar
¼ cup fresh lemon juice
2 cloves garlic, crushed

1 tablespoon dry mustard
1 teaspoon sugar (if desired)
1 tablespoon salt
Freshly ground pepper

Put all ingredients in large Mason jar, cover, shake vigorously and put in refrigerator. (Some people *do* make salad dressing at the beach!)

The most famous Saturday-night beach barbecue I have ever attended was Shad's Washtub Jambolaya (Shad was a famous cook—not the fish). Some night, when you want to impress the crowd, try his Jambolaya.

Shad's Night Beach Barbecue (Serves up to 24)

SHAD'S WASHTUB JAMBOLAYA
FRENCH BREAD
MARINATED FRUIT IN WATERMELON
PLATTER OF CHEESES
COFFEE

TO SERVE:

Beer of your choice
   or
Wente Brothers, Pinot Chardonnay, (California)
   or
"Blue Nun," Liebfraumilch (German)

Shad's Washtub Jambolaya (Serves up to 24)

24 medium-size potatoes (white rose if possible)
2 dozen lemons
48 medium yellow onions, peeled and halved
1 large bottle sauterne or any dry white wine
5 dozen jumbo shrimp, unshelled
6 pounds white sea bass, cut in chunks
12 tomatoes

2 packages of "Crab and Shrimp Boil" spices (You can't operate without this, so if you can't find it, write to the McCormick spice people in San Francisco or Baltimore and they will send it to you. In the box is a small bag to put the spices in. Do *not* use the bag—pour the spices into the boiling water.)

Dig a pit in the sand and build a fire of briquettes. Put a grill over the top. When the coals are ready, put the washtub onto the grill. Put in the tub:

The potatoes, whole, washed but *un*peeled

The onions, halved and skinned

The lemons, cut in half with all the juice and the skins tossed in. (Don't question. It gets worse.)

Enough water to cover

The packages of Crab and Shrimp Boil. (If you really can't stand hot things, use just one box of "Boil.")

Let all this boil for about 40 minutes. The potatoes should feel soft but still firm to a fork prick. Next toss in the shrimp, sea bass and halved tomatoes and the wine. Continue cooking for 20 minutes. (This will add up to an hour of total cooking time.)

To serve, spoon an assortment of goodies on each plate with a slotted spoon. The potatoes will have soaked up the hot liquid—and *wow!*

FRENCH BREAD: 4 loaves of French bread to sop up the sauce. Doesn't have to be heated, but it should be buttered and sliced part way through the loaf. Let each diner pull off a slice.

Marinated Fruit in Watermelon

2 ripe watermelons
4 peaches
6 plums
2 boxes strawberries

4 cantaloupe
1 pint each: raspberry, pineapple, mint, tangerine sherbets or reasonable facsimile thereof

1 cup Cointreau

Select ripe, attractive watermelons of medium size and prepare afternoon of the party. Turn watermelons on end and use a long narrow-bladed knife to cut off one end about a quarter of the way down, making a scalloped or notched edge. (It's hard to cut straight.) The cut-off piece becomes the lid. Scoop out the ripe insides with a big spoon and later cut them up with a melon baller. Chill the melon. Cut up enough fresh fruit to fill each watermelon about ⅔ full. Store in refrigerator. The night before party make sherbet balls with a small ice cream scoop and store in freezer.

To serve, mix the fruit with the Cointreau, fill the watermelon, put the sherbet in next, then cover with the lid. Place on a bed of crushed ice. Another washtub, filled with ice will work fine. On a moderately warm day you can count on the pre-frozen sherbet remaining firm for a half hour to an hour. If you don't want to worry about the sherbet, plan on enough fruit to fill the watermelon and forget the sherbet. But do try to keep the watermelon cold. Leftover watermelon can be used to refill watermelon.

With this dessert Shad insists on a platter of assorted fine cheeses.

Clam-Digging Weekend for Four

STEAMED CLAMS
RICE-AND-SOUR-CREAM CASSEROLE
HERBED BREAD
TOSSED SALAD
APPLE BETTY PIE
NEW ENGLAND RUM AND COFFEE

TO SERVE:

Stony Hill, Pinot Chardonnay (California)
or
Louis Jadot, Corton Charlemagne (French)
or
Louis Martini, Jugs of Mt. White (California)
or
Gallo, Chablis Blanc (California)

Steamed Clams

4 dozen clams, give or take	1 to 2 cups sherry
Cornmeal	2 cups (about) cut-up celery tops
6 peppercorns	2 bunches green onions, whole
1 tablespoon seasoned salt	Lemon Juice

Butter

Buy or dig your clams the day before you use them. Place them in a bucket of cold water and toss in a handful of cornmeal. This does something to the little dears that makes them spit out all that sand they've been stowing away.

When ready to cook, put the clams in the sink and scrub them with a brush. (Look for empty shells full of mud that can fool you into thinking they are clams.) Use a large pot with a lid and a rack in the bottom that will hold the clams at least 3 inches above the liquid. In the bottom of the pot, put the peppercorns, seasoning and sherry. Add enough water to bring the liquid just below the level of the rack. Put clams on the rack, cover with the celery tops and the onions. Put the lid on tight, place over high heat and steam for 20 minutes. The clams will open. Lift them out with tongs and serve in bowls with lemon juice and butter, equal amounts of each. (Some clams *don't* open. You can discard or pry them open with a knife and fork. They're still good.

Rice and Sour-cream Casserole   (Serves 4 to 6)

6 ounces Monterey Jack cheese or Munster
1 small carton sour cream
1 4-ounce can of chopped green chilies (In Mexican food section of market or gourmet shelves)

1½ cups cooked rice
Salt and pepper to taste
¼ cup grated Cheddar cheese

Cut the Jack cheese into thin strips. Mix the sour cream with the chopped chilies and add salt and pepper. Butter a casserole and layer it with cooked rice, the sour-cream mixture and the cheese until the casserole is full. End with rice on top. Bake in 350° F. oven for ½ hour. Sprinkle grated Cheddar cheese on top and return to hot oven until cheese melts.

Herb Bread   (Serves 4 to 6)

1 loaf bakery bread, unsliced
¼ pound soft butter

¼ teaspoon each oregano, rosemary and thyme
2 tablespoons chopped parsley

Cut off all except bottom crusts from bread. Cut the bread in thick slices, but not all the way through the bottom crust. Mix butter with the herbs and parsley and butter both sides of each piece. Wrap loaf in foil and heat in 350° F. oven for 15 to 20 minutes.

Apple Betty Pie   (Serves 4 to 6)

3 cups flour
½ cup butter
3 tablespoons sugar
4 egg yolks
1½ tablespoons lemon juice

1 tablespoon sour cream
7 cups apple slices, tart
1 cup sugar
2 teaspoons cinnamon
¾ cup fine-chopped walnuts

Blend the flour and butter together as for piecrust. Add three tablespoons of sugar, the yolks, lemon juice and sour cream. Divide dough in half. Roll one piece and fit it into a 9-inch square pan, coming up the sides with it. (You may need more than half the dough for this.)

Mix the apples with sugar and cinnamon and put half into the pan, then a layer of nuts, then rest of apples. Roll out other piece of dough and fit over the top. Seal edges as well as possible. Bake in 375° F. oven for 45 minutes or until crust is brown.

Make ahead and take with you.

Cooking at the lake is like cooking at the beach—except that it's more difficult. The markets are usually a fair distance away and the guests are just as unpredictable. Barbecuing, again, should be the chief means of entertaining.

Barbecue for Twenty

BARBECUED MEAT LOAF
BEST-EVER BAKED BEANS
HIGGINS LAKE SALAD
WATERMELON
COOKIES

You can expand this menu to feed as many as you can count, afford, or are stuck with.

TO SERVE:

Beer
   or
Barolo from Piedmont (Italian)
   or
Charles Krug, Claret (California)
   or
Louis Martini, Jugs of Mt. Burgundy (California)

Barbecued Meat Loaf   (To serve 20 make 3 loaves.)

Here are the ingredients for making 1:

1½ pounds ground chuck
1½ cups fresh bread crumbs
½ an 8-ounce can tomato sauce
1 egg, slightly beaten
1 onion, chopped
1 tablespoon Worcestershire
   sauce

2 teaspoons dry mustard
Seasoned salt and pepper to taste
1 clove garlic
½ teaspoon oregano
¼ teaspoon sage

Combine everything and form into a loaf. Place on a Pyrex cake pan and bake for 1 hour at 350° F. Chill until ready to use.

Cut loaf into 1½-inch slices and barbecue about three inches from coals. Use a wire hot-dog rack if you have one. Serve with sauce.

Sauce

2½ cans tomato sauce (see how things work out!)

¼ cup brown sugar
2 teaspoons Worcestershire sauce

Combine and simmer for a few minutes. Use to baste meat while it cooks and then pour over when you serve the meat.

Best-ever Baked Beans   (Serves 20)

2 tablespoons bacon fat
2 onions, chopped
3 green peppers, cut in chunks
1 pound mushrooms, sliced
2 large cans pork and beans
2 large cans butter beans, drained
1 pound bacon, cut into half slices

1 cup catsup
½ cup prepared mustard
1¼ cups maple syrup
2 teaspoons oregano
16 whole cloves
4 bay leaves

Put bacon fat in a large, deep pot. (Or use two medium size pots and divide ingredients.) Sauté the onions, pepper chunks and mushrooms until they are barely soft. Add everything else, mix and bake 30 to 45 minutes at 250° F. Don't be alarmed by these amounts—they'll disappear right down to the last bean.

(Be sure to cut this recipe in half when feeding 8 to 10. It's one of the best recipes in the book, so don't wait for a large crowd to try it.)

Higgins Lake Salad   (Serves 20)

6 tomatoes, sliced
4 Bermuda onions, sliced

2 cucumbers, peeled and sliced
4 navel oranges, peeled and sliced

Prepare ahead and mix. Take your two largest wooden bowls and divide the above ingredients between the two.

Dribble a good bottled oil-and-vinegar dressing over the top. The oranges are a new taste after going steady with the onions.

A nice way to spend Sunday morning is at a brunch. Gather the Sunday papers, put all the food on trays, invite the couple next door, head for the dock, dangle your feet in the cold water, play bridge. . . .

Sunday Brunch for Four

CHILLED FRUIT TRAY
CHEESE BLINTZES WITH SOUR CREAM AND STRAWBERRIES
BREAKFAST SAUSAGES
COFFEE

TO SERVE: (Before—during—and after breakfast)
Almadén, Extra Dry Champagne (California)
   or
André, Cold Duck (California)
   or
C'est Bon, Champagne, Extra Dry (California)

Chilled Fruit Tray

Cut a cantaloupe, honeydew, or other melon in narrow wedges. Wash a pound of white seedless grapes and leave in small clusters. Peel and section an orange. Peel and quarter a peach. Arrange attractively on a tray and decorate with fresh flowers.

Cheese Blintzes   (Serves 4)

BATTER:

3 eggs
1 cup milk
½ teaspoon salt

1 tablespoon salad oil
¾ cup unsifted flour
Butter for frying

TOPPING:

1 small carton sour cream
1 box strawberries, sliced (or strawberry preserves)

Beat the eggs, milk, salt and salad oil together. Stir the unsifted flour into egg mixture until well blended. Heat about 1 teaspoon butter in large iron skillet and pour ¼ cup of the batter into it, tilting the pan so batter spreads as thin as it will go. Cook on one side only over a medium-high heat until batter congeals. Bottom should be lightly browned. Stack the cakes, bottom (brown) side up, on a heated plate or lay them out on a tea towel.

When all cakes are ready, put about ¼ cup of the cheese filling (recipe below) in the center of each. Fold both sides of cake over filling. Arrange in a well-buttered heat-proof dish and place in a hot (425° F.) oven until brown (about 10 minutes). Cover with foil and put on tray.

FILLING:

2 cups drained small-curd cottage cheese	1 egg yolk
	2 tablespoons sugar
1 tablespoon lemon juice	

In a small bowl combine the cheese, egg yolk, sugar and lemon juice until very well blended.

To serve, put a spoonful of sour cream on top of each blintze and spoon on sliced strawberries or strawberry preserves. Cherry preserves are also good.

Before closing the lake cottage for the winter, plan an End-of-Season Cocktail Party. Use up the odds and ends of all liquor and keep the food simple.

End-of-season Cocktail Party

ODDS AND ENDS OF BOTTLED GOODS
BAKED HAM WITH MUSTARD
COLD MELON SURPRISE

TO SERVE:

Charles Krug, Traminer (California)
    or
Almadén, Chenin Blanc (California)
    or
Italian Swiss Colony, Chablis (California)

Baked Ham

Don't buy canned hams unless there is no choice. The ham with the bone in it that you buy at the meat counter is far better. Dip whole cloves (about 2 dozen) in nutmeg and stick in ham. Dribble a mixture of equal parts of honey, orange juice and sherry over the top. Bake about 1 to 2 hours in medium oven. Time depends on size of ham. Slice. Serve with following sauce.

Mustard Sauce for Ham

3 eggs
1 teaspoon dry mustard
1 cup brown sugar

1 tablespoon flour
½ cup mild vinegar
½ cup water

3 tablespoons butter

Beat eggs in saucepan. Mix mustard, sugar and flour together. Add vinegar, water and butter to mustard mixture and blend well. Add to eggs. Cook and stir over slow heat for 10 minutes.

Cold Melon Surprise   (Always good with ham or steak.)

2 cantaloupes
1 honeydew melon
1 tablespoon powdered sugar

Sauterne, dry white wine, or "flat"
    champagne
1 pint lemon sherbet

½ pound seedless grapes

Cut from top of each cantaloupe a plug large enough to get a spoon in to remove seeds. Stand cantaloupes securely in small bowls and sprinkle powdered sugar into cavities of each. Scoop enough melon balls from honeydew to fill the cantaloupes, then pour in sauterne until all space is used up. Chill for several hours.

To serve, drain the melon balls and the wine from cantaloupe into bowl. Spoon melon balls onto each piece of cantaloupe. Cut cantaloupe into serving pieces. Add a scoop of sherbet, cluster of grapes and pour wine over all. This makes about 8 servings, so increase as needed.

If you are invited by a man to go camping . . . don't. Even if he is your husband. Do leave something to the man alone. If, however, he offers you a mountain cabin with running water, something to cook on *and* inside plumbing—ah, well, that's another story.

Trout Breakfast

TROUT, PANFRIED (if under 6 to 8 inches.
If larger, save for dinner.)
SCRAMBLED EGGS
HOT BISCUITS
COFFEE

TO SERVE:

André, Sparkling Rosé (California)
or
Korbel, Brut Champagne (California)

(Why *not* champagne for breakfast? You're on vacation!)

Trout   (Panfried)

First rule of the house: He who caught it, cleans it!

Pepper the fish, then drop into a paper bag of flour and salt (or biscuit mix) as you would for fried chicken. Sauté in iron skillet in bacon fat over high heat until the eyes pop. (Well, he's your pioneer loved one!) Put a lemon wedge on each plate.

Trout Dinner for 6

TROUT IN CORN HUSKS
BARBECUED FRESH CORN
SPINACH AND ONION SALAD
APPLESAUCE CAKE
COFFEE

TO SERVE:

Almadén, Gewürztraminer (California)
or
Souverain, Johannesberg Riesling (California)
or
Gallo, Chablis Blanc (California)

Trout in Corn Husks

In the cavity of the cleaned trout, put a pat of butter, then give a good squeeze of lemon. Sprinkle with salt and ground pepper. Wrap each trout in a de-silked corn husk (see below) and tie the open end with string. If husks are dry, soak in water for 5 minutes before wrapping fish. Place on bed of hot coals, cover with more hot coals and cook for 15 minutes. Fish should flake when touched with a fork. Serve with sliced lemon and soft butter.

Barbecued Fresh Corn   (1 or 2 ears per person)

Carefully shuck the corn and save the husks (naturally) to wrap the trout in. Wrap the corn in foil after you butter, salt and pepper it; then put it on the coals. Keep turning. Cooks in 10 to 20 minutes. Corn will cook in 10 minutes if left unwrapped and put directly on grill.

Spinach and Onion Salad   (Serves 6)

1 pound spinach, washed, cut in pieces	¼ cup diced celery
	4 hard-boiled eggs, sliced*
1 Bermuda onion, sliced	Salt

Pepper

In a large bowl combine the spinach, onion, celery, eggs and seasoning. Refrigerate while you make dressing.

Dressing

1 small carton sour cream	Juice of 1 lemon
1 package Good Seasons garlic-cheese dry mix salad dressing	

Mix and toss with salad. If it looks like too much dressing for the amount of spinach, save and use as a marinade for thin-sliced cucumbers. Allow one bunch spinach for every three people.

Applesauce Cake   (Done ahead)

2 cups sugar	½ teaspoon cloves
½ teaspoon salt	½ teaspoon nutmeg
¾ cup shortening	½ teaspoon cinnamon
4 eggs, separated	½ teaspoon allspice
1 teaspoon grated lemon peel	1 15-ounce jar or can of apple-sauce
3¼ cups sifted flour	
1½ teaspoons baking powder	1 cup chopped walnuts
1 teaspoon soda	1 cup raisins

Cream together 1⅔ cups sugar, salt and shortening until fluffy. Beat in egg yolks, one at a time until light and fluffy. Add lemon peel. Sift together flour, baking powder, soda, cloves, nutmeg, cinnamon and allspice. Add flour mixture to egg mixture gradually, blending well after each addition. Add nuts and raisins and mix lightly.

* Take at least a dozen hard-cooked eggs with you. It is difficult to boil water in the high mountain altitudes and you may need some for a picnic lunch.

Beat egg whites at high speed until stiff but not dry. Beat in remaining ⅓ cup sugar, 1 tablespoon at a time. Fold lightly into batter. Turn into greased and floured 10-inch tube pan. Bake at 325° F. for 1 hour and 15 minutes or until a straw comes out clean.

Turn cake out onto wire rack and cool. Store in airtight container one or more days before serving. Make at least one day before you leave for the mountains. Now, don't you feel organized?

Barbecue for Eight

BARBECUED STEELHEAD TROUT
VEGETABLE CASSEROLE
RED-CABBAGE SLAW
BARBECUED APPLES
COFFEE

TO SERVE:

Freemark Abbey, Pinot Chardonnay (A new California wine)
    or
Charles Krug, Chenin Blanc (California)
    or
Beaulieu Vineyard, Pinot Chardonnay (California)

Barbecued Steelhead Trout   (Serves 8)

1 steelhead trout (about 5 pounds)	1 large onion, sliced
2 teaspoons salt	3 sprigs parsley
½ teaspoon pepper	3 celery tops
1 clove garlic, mashed	1 green pepper, sliced

10 slices bacon

Rub fish inside and out with salt and pepper, then with garlic. Mix the vegetables and use them to stuff fish. Put bacon under and over fish and wrap foil around it to hold the whole thing in place. Put on grill and cook for 1½ hours. Throw away the vegetables. They draw the taste out of the fish and will therefore taste fishy. Cook a shorter time for a smaller fish and a longer time for a larger fish. (What could be more basic than that?)

NOTE: A steelhead trout is a "gamey" fish—tough to catch and tough to eat. But barbecued it isn't so bad. Since it takes a while to cook, have your fisherman build the fire before he goes to clean up. You can use this method of cooking fish for any really fishy-tasting fish.

Vegetable Casserole   (Serves 8)

1 box frozen chopped spinach, cooked and drained
1 8-ounce package medium noodles
¼ pound butter
½ pound fresh mushrooms, sliced
3 small carrots, peeled and sliced thin
½ cup chopped parsley
1 pound Velveeta or any processed American cheese

Put spinach on to cook according to directions. Put noodles on to cook but only boil them 6 minutes. In a large iron skillet melt the butter and sauté the other vegetables. While everything cooks, grate the cheese. Cold cheese grates best. As each item is finished cooking, put it in a large casserole with a lid. Mix all together and bake for 30 minutes in a moderate oven (350° F.). This excellent casserole can be made ahead and reheated.

Red-cabbage Slaw   (Serves 8)

4 cups shredded red cabbage
1 small cauliflower, raw and cut up
1 cup chopped celery
6 green onions, chopped, including tops

Mix altogether and add the following dressing:

2 tablespoons sugar
2 teaspoons salt
⅔ cup olive oil or salad oil
6 tablespoons tarragon vinegar

Put salad oil in small mixing bowl. Add vinegar a few drops at a time. Beat well with a fork after each addition. Beat in sugar and salt a teaspoon at a time. Pour over vegetables.

Barbecued Apples

1 apple per person
Raisins—1 tablespoon per apple
Sack of cinnamon candies (Red Hots)
Butter

Core each apple and place on a square of foil. Fill the hollow with 1 tablespoon raisins and 1 tablespoon candies mixed together. Dot with butter. Bring foil up loosely over apples and twist ends together to seal. Grill on barbecue for about 30 minutes.

Crawfish (Crayfish)

Something to look for in your mountain stream is crawfish. They look like miniature lobsters with two front claws. (In France they're called *ecrevisses*.) The best way to catch them is with a piece of meat tied onto a string. Lower the meat (liver seems to work best) down between the rocks to lure the crawfish. Once one grabs hold, gently pull him up, slide a net under and shake him loose. Then dump him into a burlap bag. When you have about 20 to 30, head home.

Back at the cabin put the crawfish in a tub of water to keep them alive until you're ready to cook them. Build a fire and put a tub of water on to boil (about 3 quarts). Add 5 tablespoons of salt and some fresh dill if you can find it. If not, use dried. Also add two cans of beer.

The next step is the cleaning. Ugh! Get your man to do it, if you can. If you do it, grasp the live crayfish behind his pincers and turn him over. You'll see that the tip of his tail is in three sections. If you twist the center section and pull gently, the sand vein comes out easily. As you clean each one, put it into another pail of water so you won't lose track. When they are all clean, drain off as much as you can of the water, then dump into the boiling tub of water and beer. Boil for about 6 to 8 minutes. Remove the tub from the fire and let it stand until cooled. Take the little fellows out and chill, if you have the time. If not, serve them when cool enough to handle. Served with some mayonnaise they are a perfect hot hors d'oeuvre. Or you can dig out the meat and serve in a salad or mixed with rice as a main-course dish.

Mountain Mexican Lunch for Six

CHILIES RELLENOS CON QUESO
GUACAMOLE SALAD
CORN CHIPS

TO SERVE:
Cold Beer

Lunch in the mountains depends on where you are and what you're doing. If the fishing is bad and you've been doing a jigsaw puzzle all morning, do something a bit different for lunch.

Chilies Rellenos Con Queso (Serves 6)

The following ingredients are items you would normally have, plus a few canned things you can plan to take along just in case.

1 can green chilies, whole (Ortega brand if available)
1 cup sharp cheese, grated
Flour
6 egg whites
6 egg yolks
3 tablespoons flour

Salt
Salad oil
1 can salsa or enchilada sauce (Ortega usually has a shelf of Mexican food in the supermarket)

Cut chilies in half, crossways. Stuff with cheese. Roll in flour.

Beat egg whites until stiff but not dry. Beat yolks until lemon-colored and add 3 tablespoons flour and dash of salt. Fold this into whites.

Heat about ¼ inch of salad oil in a small frying pan. For each *relleno* mound about ½ cup egg mixture in pan. As batter begins to set, gently top the mound with a stuffed chili. Cover with more batter and cook until bottom is nicely browned. Carefully turn and brown other side. Put in paper towel lined pan and keep warm in oven. Serve with the sauce, heated.

Guacamole Salad (Serves 6)

2 ripe avocados
2 tablespoons lemon juice
2 tablespoons grated onion

2 cloves garlic, crushed
½ teaspoon salt
½ teaspoon coarse ground pepper

½ tablespoon of the salsa you are using on rellenos

GARNISH:

1 tomato, cut in wedges
2 hard-cooked eggs, quartered

1 sack of corn chips

Peel and mash avocados. Add remaining ingredients. Put the avocado in a mound in the center of a platter. Surround with tomato wedges, sliced hard-boiled eggs and corn chips.

V

Riding or Flying

A Hunt Breakfast, dear, is not something you eat before the ride, or you wouldn't make it over the first fence. If, like Auntie Mame, you can't ride, but happen to cotton to a houndsman, don't ride. Fix this breakfast instead. (Or just invite twelve people to breakfast to watch the Kentucky Derby on TV).

Hunt Breakfast for Twelve

FRENCH 75'S
FRESH FRUIT ARRAY
SCRAMBLED EGGS, CHICKEN LIVERS AND MUSHROOMS
HOT ORANGE ROLLS
COFFEE

French 75's

Absolutely guaranteed to dissolve all pain. (Also complexes, sensitivities, inhibitions and hang-ups.)

Plan to serve French 75's from a large cut-glass or silver punch bowl. Assemble your ingredients next to it. At the last minute, as you hear the hounds fill bowl ⅔ full of ice cubes. Mix following ingredients (except orange) and pour over ice in the bowl.

3 dashes bitters   ½ cup brandy
3 twists of lemon peel

Then toss in

1 large bottle Demi-sec champagne* chilled	12 thin slices of orange with rind

Ladle into champagne glasses and garnish with orange slices. This recipe is for twelve single servings. If you double the recipe, don't complain that no one warned you about the effects from a French 75!

Scrambled Eggs

Allow 2 eggs per person. Crack into a bowl and beat. Scramble in a skillet at the last minute and transfer to a covered chafing dish. Place over a very low flame. Season eggs of course. If you are a veteran chafing dish user, scramble eggs right on the braizer. I find it's easier to do them the conventional way, however.

Chicken Livers and Mushrooms

2½ pounds fresh chicken livers	1 cup dry white wine
¼ cup flour	2 chicken-bouillon cubes dissolved in 1 cup boiling water
1 stick butter (¼ pound)	
½ onion, minced	1 bay leaf
½ green pepper, chopped	Pinch thyme
2 tbsp. fresh chopped parsley	Pinch nutmeg
1 pound fresh mushrooms, thinly sliced or 2 cans	½ 8 ounce package sliced almonds

Put the chicken livers in a paper bag with flour. Shake.

Melt butter in heavy iron skillet and sauté livers, onion, green pepper, parsley and mushrooms. When the livers are nicely brown, add the wine and dissolved bouillon, stirring constantly. Add bay leaf and thyme. Cover and simmer for 10 to 15 minutes. Reheat just before serving. Pour into a chafing dish, sprinkle with dash nutmeg and almonds.

Set next to the chafing dish containing scrambled eggs (above) so each person can put the chicken and mushrooms on his eggs or not, as he prefers.

* Just to add to your knowledge of things drinkable, champagne comes as *Brut* (very dry), *Sec* (semi-dry) and *Doux* (sweet). See wine chapter at back of book for more complete details.

Hot Orange Rolls   (16 rolls)

½ cup brown sugar, firmly
  packed
2 tablespoons frozen orange juice,
  concentrate

2 tablespoons butter, melted
¼ teaspoon cinnamon
2 packages (8 each) refrigerator
  flaky rolls

In bowl combine the sugar, juice concentrate, butter and cinnamon until well mixed. Spread 2 tablespoons of mixture in bottom of each of 16 muffin tins. Place roll in each cup.

Bake in a moderately hot oven (375° F.) for 8 to 10 minutes, or until rolls look brown. (Another way is to stand two rolls up in each muffin cup and make a double roll. If you do this, bake 15 to 18 minutes.)

Allow to stand in the pan 2 or 3 minutes, then turn upside down on plate and serve. (I am assuming you already have figured out that to turn anything as runny and sticky as these, you invert the plate on top of the muffin tin, grasp the two together and turn.)

If the Hunt is held some distance from your kitchen you may choose to pack a lunch and go along as a Hilltopper.

Under-the-tree Picnic for Two

CUCUMBER AND BERMUDA ONION SANDWICHES
COLD CRAB AND RICE SALAD
TINY PASTRIES

TO SERVE:

Taittinger, Blanc de Blancs Champagne (French)
  or
Paul Masson, Brut Champagne (California)
  or
André, Pink Champagne (California)
Serve in glass champagne glasses

In the ice chest lay the previously chilled champagne flat and cover with ice packs. (These are plastic bags with a chemical inside. You can buy them at a hardware store. They are about the size of an ice tray. Freeze solid then transfer to cold chest.)

Next, arrange the sandwich makings and the salad in the cold chest and save a corner for the pastries and the champagne glasses.

Cucumber and Bermuda Onion Sandwiches

Take black bread in a plastic bag and a carton of real butter. In another plastic bag put thin, thin slices of onion and cucumber. Build the sandwiches after you arrive. And why not splurge on a tiny jar of real caviar to have with the champagne?

Cold Crab and Rice Salad   (Serves 2)

⅓ pound fresh crab meat (or canned if not available fresh)
1½ cups cold cooked rice
2 tablespoons French dressing
¼ cup mayonnaise

2 tablespoons minced onion
2 teaspoons anchovy paste
½ teaspoon dry mustard
¾ cup sliced celery
2 tablespoons minced parsley

2 large tomatoes

Pick over the crab meat for bits of shell. Combine with rice and French dressing. Marinate in refrigerator for 30 minutes. Combine rest of ingredients except tomatoes, and mix with crab meat and rice. Refrigerate. Slice off tops of the tomatoes and scoop out the insides. Turn upside down on paper towel lined dish to drain and put in refrigerator to chill.

Just before leaving the house, stuff the tomatoes with the crab salad, wrap in plastic and pack.

PASTRIES: Buy two lovely tiny gooeys at Ye Favorite Bake Shoppe.

So many men own planes nowadays that it's not uncommon to be married to or courted by a man who flies. (A plane, that is.) But since only a handful of men own planes on which you can prepare food, this "plane" fare includes things you pack in a hamper.

Things Packable (For short outings)

(See "Tailgating" for more elaborate fare.)

CHEESES: Pack the cheeses in foil. Take a knife for paring.

HARD ROLLS: Buy good bakery French rolls. Or take a tin of water biscuits or carton of soda crackers.

ICED TEA: Make triple strength tea from leaves brewed in a teapot. Put into thermos with ice cubes and take along sugar and lemon.

FRUIT: Grapes, tangerines, apples, oranges, anything fresh and ripe.

A good copilot always has a little sack of snacks to eat while in the air, both coming and going. Make up a packet from this list. Chocolate bars, gum, nuts, raisins, dry fruits, dates, Life Savers and cookies.

Be careful not to choose things that are too salty. And take your thermos to the nearest coffee shop and have it filled with fresh coffee for the trip back home. And never include anything alcoholic!

VI

Food Afloat

"... and this is the galley!"

If your husband (or your beau, or your best friend's husband) is a boat owner, you are probably only too aware that "The galley, Mate, is where, on a boat, you cook at!" In the best interests of all concerned, there is but *one* cook. And if it's you, make this clear to all aboard: *You* plan the meals, *you* shop, *you* stow the food . . . and *you* are the only one with access to the refrigerator.

Do everything you can before the morning lines are cast off. And this includes cooking several things at home and bringing them aboard ready to eat. Most boats now have a barbecue unit that fits over the stern or that can be assembled on an open deck. However, you obviously can't barbecue under way, so plan at least one precooked casserole that can be reheated.

Canned foods are your best friends, especially soups. They can be stored under bunks, under seats, anywhere that's under. If you put them *up* anyplace, be sure they are secure. Buy your drinks in cans; also juices, vegetables, extra fruits, some meat and potatoes. Take as much fresh fruit as you can. Also, take a couple dozen hard-boiled eggs.

Wash all your salad "makings," dry in towel, and take them on board in plastic bags. Don't separate the lettuce leaves or cut off the green-onion ends, but do top the radishes. Wash and bag carrots. Forget fresh celery, it takes up too much room. Bring a green pepper and some tomatoes and leave them out of refrigerator with fruit. Bring a whole fresh pineapple, also.

When cooking on top of the stove, watch everything carefully. Even with guard rails, pots and pans can bounce and slide around. Be sure the oven has an outside latch. Dishwashing is to be avoided because there is always a limited fresh-water supply. So line pots and pans with foil or use the disposable ones. The same with dishes; use paper or plastic.

As for things alcoholic? Since Captains have kept logs, liquor has had a history. As the cook, it's your duty to have plenty of "go withs." Ice is another matter. When in port, you have a "detail" who go ashore for a plastic bagful.

My final word to all you sea cooks is: Remember that under way the cook's prowess and the crew's retentive powers are dictated by the Sea and Swell Scale. So don't be a hero. Nobody loves a sick cook. . . .

Let's handle the menus all at once for this section so that you can plan what to buy, what to supply:

MENUS FOR A WEEKEND IN THE COVE FOR SIX LUCKY PEOPLE

Friday Lunch Under Way

CARELESS MATADORS
HOT VICHYSSOISE IN MUGS
COLD FRIED CHICKEN
PINEAPPLE SLAW
COOKIES
COFFEE

TO SERVE:

Korbel, Brut Champagne (California)
> or

Charles Krug, Johannisberg Reisling (California)
> or

Chateau Margaux 1964 (French)

Friday Cocktail Hour

VODKA- OR GIN-AND-TONICS (OR MARTINIS)
MARINATED MUSHROOMS
SHRIMP SI SI

Friday Dinner in the Cove

BARBEQUED STEAK TERIYAKI
RICE
TOSSED SALAD
HOT MILK CAKE
COFFEE

TO SERVE:

Masamune Såké (Japanese)
or
Inglenook, Cabernet Sauvignon (California)
or
Paul Masson, Gamay Beaujolais (California)

Saturday Breakfast

SCREWDRIVERS
HALF CANTELOPE WITH BERRIES
SWEET ROLLS (Packaged)
EGGS-TO-ORDER-ON-REQUEST

Saturday Lunch

OCEAN MOTION
AVOCADO SALAD WITH CONSOMMÉ
GOLDEN SANDWICHES
FRUIT
COOKIES

Saturday Cocktail Hour

MAI TAIS
HOT MUSHROOM BOUCHÉES
SPICED OLIVES

Saturday Night Dinner

TOP SIRLOIN, BARBECUED
VEGETABLE-RICE BUNDLES
CELERY VICTOR
HOT ROLLS
GRILLED BROWNWICHES
COFFEE

TO SERVE:

Louis Martini, Cabernet Sauvignon (California)
or
Inglenook, Pinot Noir (California)
or
Egri Bikauer, Hungarian Bull's Blood

Sunday Breakfast

SALTY DOGS
FRUIT COMPOTE
PANCAKES WITH SOUR CREAM AND BLACKBERRY SYRUP
SAUSAGES

Sunday Lunch

BLOODY MARYS
HOT SOUP (Whatever kind available)
PLATTER OF LEFTOVERS FOR SANDWICHES

Sunday Dinner

Dinner Sunday night is in port, after the trip home. Let it be in the nearest restaurant!

Careless Matador   (Serves 4)

1 can beef bouillon   Tomato juice
Vodka

Into a pitcher, about the size you use when you make up a can of frozen orange juice, pour the beef bouillon. Add a soup can of tomato juice and a can of vodka. Place ice in double Old Fashioned glasses and pour on the mixture. Season with a squeeze of lemon and dash of Tabasco.

Hot Vichyssoise   (Serves 6)

2 leeks
2 tablespoons butter
1½ cups thin sliced potatoes
1 can chicken broth

2 teaspoons sugar
½ teaspoon salt
¼ teaspoon pepper
1 cup cereal cream or ½ and ½
1 cup whipping cream

Remove the green tops from the leeks and slice the white part into thin slices. Using a saucepan, sauté in the butter for 5 minutes, then add the potatoes and chicken broth. Cook, uncovered, over medium heat for about 25 minutes or until potatoes are tender.

Put half the mixture in blender and mix. Repeat with the other half. Pour each half, after mixing, back into the saucepan. Add the rest of the ingredients, heat and then put in thermos. Serve as hot as the thermos will keep it. It is equally good chilled.

Make ahead of time and take in thermos.

Cold Fried Chicken

Either fry by your favorite recipe the day before you leave, or buy from one of the good drive-in places that seem to be on every street corner.

Pineapple Slaw   (Serves 6)

1 cabbage, finely shredded
½ green pepper, chopped
¼ small can pimientos, chopped
1 small can pineapple tidbits, drained

½ cup mayonnaise
1 tablespoon lime juice
½ teaspoon dry mustard
1 teaspoon celery seeds

Mix the cabbage, pepper and pimientos. Drain pineapple and add. Blend rest of ingredients and add to cabbage mixture. Make ahead of time and keep in covered bowl. If you plan to eat as soon as you're under way, you don't need to refrigerate the chicken or the salad.

COOKIES: Buy package of best bakery variety.

COFFEE: Make and take in thermos. Then you won't have to light stove for the entire trip over.

After you are securely moored, you may want to swim or water-ski before dinner. But be sure you get the men to set up the barbecue before they go overboard. Start the cocktail hour whenever you get a volunteer.

Marinated Mushrooms   (Done at home.)

1 pound small white fresh mush-
rooms

Small bottle vinegar-and-oil dressing
Sauterne or any dry white wine

Wash mushrooms and take out the stems. Marinate in a bowl in the dressing.

Before you leave, pour the dressing into a jar and save for a steak marinade at home, later. Put the mushrooms into a plastic jar with a tight lid and cover with sauterne or white wine.

Shrimp Si Si

1 cup bottled barbecue sauce
3 tablespoons lemon juice
1 tablespoon Worcestershire sauce

1 pound fresh shrimp, peeled and
cleaned

Combine the first three ingredients. Put shrimp into heavy plastic bag and pour the marinade over them. Tie securely and take aboard like this. Refrigerate until the cocktail hour. Grill the shrimp as you wait for the fire to settle for the steak. The swimmers can get warm at the barbecue as they get fed. Heat the marinade and keep nearby to dip the shrimp in.

Barbecued Steak Teriyaki   (Serves 6)

Have your favorite butcher fix two eyes of fillet, unsliced, and wrap them. Take aboard and put in refrigerator. When boat is moored, take out of refrigerator and slice each fillet into individual steaks, about 1 inch thick. You can get from 6 to 8 slices from each eye. Marinate in bottled soy sauce until ready to cook. Barbecue quickly on each side. Serve rare. (Is there any other way?)

RICE: In gourmet section of your market buy packaged rice with the seasoning already in it, and follow directions. One with saffron is especially good.

Tossed Salad

Made of mixed lettuce, sliced peppers, tomato, onion, radishes—you know the rest. Mix with good bottled dressing.

Hot Milk Cake

Make this ahead of time and take on board with you.

1 cup milk	2 cups flour
2 tablespoons butter	2 teaspoons baking powder
1 teaspoon vanilla	4 eggs, beaten well
	2 cups sugar

Heat milk and butter together. Add vanilla. Sift the flour with the baking powder and slowly add to the milk mixture. Add the well beaten eggs and the sugar.

Bake in flat Pyrex pan in 350° F. oven for about 25 to 30 minutes. Cake is done when middle springs back to soft touch. Well, that's the way I learned to do it. So can you.

Frosting

10 tablespoons brown sugar	4 teaspoons milk
6 teaspoons butter	½ cup shredded coconut
	¼ cup chopped walnuts

Cook sugar, butter and milk over low heat until it spins a thread. Add coconut and nuts. Frost the cake and slip it under a hot broiler for 2 to 3 minutes. Sugar will bubble and the whole thing will kind of run together. Really a great cake if you like cake.

Screwdrivers

Orange juice and vodka on the rocks as per page 3. What a way to greet the sea!

Half Cantaloupe with Berries

Cut cantaloupe in half, scoop out the seeds and fill with washed berries.

To serve lunch, you have to have some idea of who's where, so at breakfast remember to say, "Lunch at one." Try to have a lunch with everything on one plate so the sun worshipers can eat while lounging on sun mats.

Ocean Motion   (Serves 1)

2 jiggers tomato juice   Shakes of Tabasco
1 jigger clam juice   No salt
1 jigger vodka   Hefty squeeze of lemon
                    ¼ teaspoon celery salt

Mix in cocktail shaker or pitcher and serve over ice in tall glass. When serving this at home, put in a stalk of celery as a muddler. Neat drink, on land or sea.

Avocado Salad with Consomme   (Serves 6)

3 ripe avocados   Small carton sour cream
2 cans consommé (Stow in refrig- Juice of 1 lemon
  erator on Friday night after din- Tiny jar caviar
  ner when there's more room.)   Seasoned salt
                    Seasoned pepper

Halve the avocados and remove pits but don't peel. Spoon ⅓ can jellied consommé into each half and sprinkle with lemon juice, salt and pepper. Put spoonful of sour cream on that, and then a teaspoon of caviar. (Red caviar is fine for this.)

Golden Sandwiches   (Single serving)

2 slices sourdough French bread 3 strips canned green chilies
1 thick slice Jack or Muenster   Butter
  cheese

On 1 slice of bread put cheese, on other slice put the chilies. Put together and butter the outside of each piece. Fry in butter until cheese is melted.

COOKIES: If you decide to take homemade cookies, carry them in a shoe box lined with foil and taped shut. They pack well this way and the box is a good camouflage to protect them from noshers until ready to serve.

MAI TAIS: For homemade Mai Tais see page 16. But for this trip buy a mix already made.

Serve the Mai Tais in double Old Fashioned glasses, over ice, and with a wedge of fresh pineapple stuck in. Plan to bring a whole ripe pineapple aboard. Save what you don't use now for Sunday breakfast.

Hot Mushroom Bouchees

2 tablespoons minced onion (or dehydrated)
1 cup sliced mushrooms
¼ cup butter
4 hard-boiled eggs chopped (See footnote p. 48.)

2 tablespoons chopped parsley
Salt
Pepper
1 egg, beaten
Packaged toast rounds
½ cup grated sharp cheese

1 box toast rounds

Sauté the onions and mushrooms in butter for 5 minutes. Add chopped hard-boiled eggs, parsley, salt and pepper. Add beaten egg and cook until thick. Put 1 tablespoon of mixture on toast rounds, sprinkle with the cheese and slip under the broiler until the cheese melts and bouchées are heated through.

Spiced Olives   (Make ahead of time)

Choose all kinds of olives for this: green or black or both. Greek, Italian or Spanish are the best. But not any stuffed olives. Buy at least 3 to 5 pints. Place in a gallon jar with a tight lid. Mix together and add:

1 tablespoon freshly ground pepper
10 cloves garlic, crushed
10 hot peppers

2 lemons sliced paper thin
3 to 4 sprigs fresh dill or 1 teaspoon dill weed
Olive oil to almost cover

Allow to stand for several days. Bring on board in the jar.

Barbecued Top Sirloin   (Serves 6)

1 piece top sirloin, 2 inches thick (Tell your butcher it's to feed 6 people.)

Olive oil
Dry mustard
Ground pepper

With knife make slashes around steak at about 2-inch intervals. Coat meat on both sides with olive oil, then with a thin coat of mustard. Sprinkle heavily with the pepper. Let stand for about 1 hour. Barbecue.

Vegetable-rice Bundles   (Serves 6)

4 to 6 ounce can water chestnuts
1 pound canned bean sprouts
3 cups cooked rice (Minute rice will do)

2 green onions, chopped with tops
½ green pepper, chopped
¼ cup buter

Cook rice according to directions on box. Drain the chestnuts and cut up. Drain the sprouts and add to chestnuts. Mix rice with onions, pepper and butter. Add to chestnuts and sprouts.

Cut 12 pieces of regular size foil about 8 inches long. Put two pieces of foil together; fit into a bowl to make a pouch. Place 2 spoonsful of mixtures into the pouch, seal edges tightly and remove from bowl. Repeat process until you have six pouches. Heat on grill in moderately warm area for 15 to 25 minutes.

To serve, roll back edges of foil and eat right from pouch.

Celery Victor   (Serves 6)

On Saturday morning put 2 medium cans of celery stalks into refrigerator. (8 ounce cans) At dinner arrange a platter of 6 lettuce cups and into each put ⅓ can of celery, drained. Sprinkle with capers and surround with quartered hard-boiled eggs. Pour bottled Italian dressing over all.

Grilled Brownwiches

Make brownies at home and pack in foil. (Use a brownie mix or recipe on back of box of chocolate.) After dinner, split each brownie in half and put a mint-filled chocolate patty between the halves. Wrap in foil and heat on barbecue until the candy melts.

Salty Dogs   (See page 6.)

Fruit Compote

To the leftover pineapple and any juice that has collected, add other cut-up fruit and mix. Place on table with paper bowls and let guests eat while they quaff their Salty Dogs.

Sausages

Cook sausages and keep warm in oven while you fix pancakes.

PANCAKES: Follow directions on mix box. Serve with warm blackberry syrup and sour cream.

Sunday late lunch is usually snacks served under way on the cruise home. Hot consommé in mugs is always welcome. Heat and put into thermos before you leave mooring. With this, serve chopped-egg-and-deviled-ham sandwiches, a salad made with whatever is left. If you are pretty well wiped out, marinate a couple of canned vegetables in French dressing for about an hour. For dessert, some cookies and a thermos of hot spiced tea.

Everyone on board a pleasure boat likes to fish or search for sea life. The trick is not so much in catching it as in what to do with it once it's presented to you. (You're the cook, remember.) Here are a few of the more unusual items that could be forced upon you.

Abalone

When triumphantly brought aboard (you must dive to catch abs), it's important that they be "shucked" while still fresh. Don't try to salvage all the meat. Trim off the brown skin and the fringe flesh around the foot. Do try to get the men to do this, *and* the pounding, which is the next step. Pound and pound and pound . . . about 5 minutes per ab.

For a sensational lunch try abalone sandwiches on sourdough bread with cold white wine.

To fry abs, dip in beaten egg and fine bread crumbs, then fry lightly in butter for 30 seconds per side. Overcooked abs taste rather like shoe leather.

TO SERVE:

Wenté, Pinot Blanc (California)
   or
Charles Krug, Traminer (California)
   or
Gallo, Rhine Garten (California)

Scallops

Scallops are delicious when "cooked" by action of citrus juice. This Mexican dish can be served icy cold in nests of lettuce or scooped-out tomatoes or avocado halves. Cut the fresh scallops into small pieces and cover with fresh lemon or lime juice. Cover and put in refrigerator for a couple of hours. When the scallops lose their translucency, they are "done." Drain and mix them with chopped green onion or chopped green chilies (canned) and serve.

Squid

You don't catch squid or octopus on purpose. They tangle themselves in your lines or lodge themselves in traps.

The small squid are actually very good to eat for all parts, except ink sack, are edible. Cut away and discard the ink sack. Boil the squid until tender. (They turn lavender.) When cool, use them in salads or chopped as a sandwich spread.

Octopus   Well, it's a delicacy in Europe.

To prepare fresh octopus, you must first clean and skin it. Slit open the head cavity and discard the interior. Cut away the beak between the legs and discard. Drop separated head and legs into rapidly boiling water and simmer, covered, for about 30 minutes. Let octopus cool in cooking water. Remove, peel and discard the skin.

If you're still with me, here is what you now do with the cooked and skinned meat:

Octopus Vinaigrette

¼ cup olive oil   ¼ cup lemon juice
                    Salt and pepper

Slice the octopus very thin and marinate for several hours in olive oil, lemon juice and seasonings. Serve as an appetizer or tossed in a green salad.

Fried Octopus

Dip pieces of cooked octopus in beaten egg, roll in fine bread crumbs, and cook in hot fat, at least 1½ inches deep, until golden brown. Drain on paper towel. Serve with lemon slices and dap of mayonnaise.

Halibut

If a halibut is brought in, grab a couple of slices to make cerviche.

Cerviche

Raw halibut (or any good, solid   1 small jar pimiento-stuffed green
    white fish)   olives, chopped
1 chopped tomato   1 tablespoon olive oil
1 chopped Bermuda onion   Salt and pepper
                     Lime juice

Scrape and clean the fish and cut into bite-size pieces. Marinate fish in lime juice to cover for 45 minutes, then add rest of ingredients. Chill and serve as an hors d'oeuvre.

I haven't mentioned crab, shrimp or lobster. They are hard to catch and in the case of lobster, illegal in some areas. If you do need to cook them, check the index as I've given excellent recipes in other chapters.

Early one summer morning, aboard a friend's boat, moored in a tiny cove in Baja, California, we were hailed from shore by two young students on a geological expedition. They had caught a wild pig and asked if we wanted it. "Luau!" went up the cry from about fourteen boats whose occupants had also heard the words, "Wild pig."

The work was divided among volunteers from the various boats. Since the pig had been caught alive, the crew that volunteered to clean and skin it had a chance to apply "inside" marinade. This was done by forcing liquor down the pig's throat. It relaxes the flesh and makes it sweeter. (Is there a message here?)

After the pig is killed, cleaned and skinned, it's soaked overnight in a big tub in this mixture, collected by the Marinade Committee from all participating boats:

Marinade

1 gallon sherry
1 botle soy sauce
2 cans frozen limeade or ½ cup bottled lime juice mixed with 2 tablespoons sugar

2 cans papayas or pineapple slices or pears
3 or 4 teaspoons powdered ginger (Root is best but hard to find)
4 cloves garlic, crushed

6 teaspoons seasoned salt

This marinade is an approximation of what we used. You can be as inventive as you like. I don't think there is a traditional pig marinade, but, of course, I could be wrong.

The Pit Committee did their digging right away because the fire had to be started early next morning. Dig at least 2 feet deep and six feet across. The pit is rock-lined and must be full of hot embers before the pig is lowered in. This is done by laying a campfire in the bottom of pit, covering with rocks and then lighting. Let burn down.

To barbecue, the pig was wrapped in leaves. I think we used banana leaves that we found ashore, but Ti leaves are traditional. Next, a clean sheet, if you can find one, is soaked in the marinade and wrapped around the pig. This is followed by a layer of burlap, also soaked. Heavy wire is wound around the burlap to hold everything in place and to use as handles.

The last step was to lower the pig into the pit and cover it with sand, until smoke was no longer visible. Here it remained until 8 or 9 or 10 P.M., I can't remember. It's better to overcook pork as you know, and a whole roast pig can cook 10 hours. But six hours is enough for a 150 pound pig.

TO SERVE:

Gallo, Chianti (California)
    or
Almadén, Grenache Rosé (California)
    or
Mirassou, Petite Sirah (California)

NOTE: I have helped skin and clean a pig, but I'm not going to tell you how to do it—if you *don't* know, you can't be pressed into service. It is interesting but not very nice. One hint you could toss out is that short, sharp knives work best in the skinning process. You hold the skin very taut in your left hand and, with the knife in your right, make short pushing strokes . . .! No! You make the salad and leave *that* to the men.

VII

Ski Food

Skiing is a sport that has a food life all it's own.

When going for a cross-country ski, pack a knapsack to take with you. If you know there are chalets along the way, take some tea bags. Make your tea by dipping snow into a pan and boiling it over the fire. If you are not sure of what you'll find along the trail, take wine sacks of cold white wine. (Take one anyway.)

If you know you can count on a stove, take along sausages, instant soup, even a hot dog. Choose the rest of the items from the list following:

Here Is a List of Good Things for a Knapsack

Oranges . . . because you become terribly thirsty on a cross-country ski.

Pears, tangerines and/or apples

Tea bags . . . The purists in Canada take loose tea and brew it in pots which I have seen hanging along the walls in the chalets.

Instant soup . . . any kind.

Hot dogs . . . to boil or fry

Sausages . . . to boil or fry

Hard rolls or pieces of thick-sliced dark bread. Soft slices don't ride well.

Cheese . . . any kind except very soft.

Crackers

English biscuits . . . You can buy these in tins in most markets.

Candy bars . . . Great afternoon energy lift

Hard-boiled eggs . . . And don't forget the salt.

Wine . . . White wine, carried over your shoulder in a sheepskin bag. To drink, put your head back, open your mouth and squeeze. Lovely! (Some sheepskin bags, however, are *not* so lovely—especially those from Egypt. They give wine a strange taste.)

A skier's day begins with breakfast, which should be something that sticks to the ribs, not the abdomen. And it should begin with fruit or fruit juice.

Aprés Ski you can go one of two ways—tea or Glühwein. You'll get the odd ones who want a cold beer or a stiff drink, but try to hold them off until cocktail time. With the tea or wine, serve pickup food. This is where cheese fondue started. (Or at least it's where it has ended.)

Ski Breakfast for Four

JUICE OR FRUIT
CREAMED EGGS
SAUSAGES
COFFEE OR TEA

Ski Breakfast for Six

JUICE OR FRUIT
BEEF LINDSTROM
HARD ROLLS
COFFEE OR TEA

Ski Breakfast for Noneaters   (There are always some)

COLD JUICE
JAM TART
MEXICAN HOT CHOCOLATE

Creamed Eggs   (Serves 4)

8 eggs
1 can asparagus soup
¼ cup milk

1 tablespoon butter
4 English muffins
Grated sharp cheese, about 1 cup

Beat the eggs and stir in the soup and milk. Melt butter in a frying pan and scramble eggs.

Split and slightly toast the muffins. Spoon eggs onto muffin halves. Sprinkle with grated cheese and put quickly under broiler. Serve immediately.

Beef Lindstrom (Serves 6)

1½ pounds very best lean beef, ground
1 cup diced cooked potatoes
1 cup diced beets (Canned are okay, but drain well.)

½ onion chopped
1 tablespoon capers
Seasoned salt and Pepper
2 teaspoons A-1 sauce
6 eggs

Mix meat with everything but the eggs. Form into patties and fry in butter. Don't overcook. Leave patties quite rare in the middle. Fry the eggs separately and put one on each patty.

Jam Tart

1 can refrigerator biscuits
½ stick butter, melted or soft
Strawberry jam

Sugar
Cinnamon

Take each biscuit and flatten it. Spread with very soft or melted butter. Sprinkle with sugar and cinnamon. Place 1 teaspoon strawberry jam in center. Fold over and press edges together to seal.

Bake on cookie sheet for 8 minutes in 425° F. oven. Makes 12 tarts.

Mexican Hot Chocolate

2 ounces unsweetened chocolate
2 tablespoons hot water
⅔ cup sugar
1 tablespoon cornstarch

½ teaspoon salt
2 teaspoons cinnamon
2 cups strong brewed coffee
3 cups milk
1 teaspoon vanilla

Put chocolate and hot water in top of double boiler. Heat until chocolate melts. Add sugar, cornstarch, salt and cinnamon. Add coffee and stir until smooth. Cook for 5 minutes then stir in milk and vanilla. Whip to a froth in an electric blender and serve hot. Really a treat.

APRÉS SKI:

Tea

or

Glühwein (Glowing Wine)

TEA: Buy excellent quality loose tea and make in a pot that has been warmed with hot water. Serve with lemon slices, milk, and sugar.

Glühwein

To a bottle of Gallo, Hearty Burgundy add:

1½ cups boiling water   ½ lemon, cut in slices
½ cup sugar   3 cinnamon sticks
        2 whole cloves (stuck in rind of lemon slices)

Heat just to boiling point, but do not boil. Serve with a dash of nutmeg.

GOOD HOT DRINKS (without wine): Since cocktails *will* be served before dinner, you may want to have a hot drink that is nonalcoholic. Here are two excellent ones:

Scandinavian Fruit Toddy   (Serves 6)

2 cans frozen pineapple-grapefruit   1 teaspoon whole cloves
  juice   2 sticks cinnamon
1 quart cold water   ⅓ cup raisins
        2 tablespoons whole blanched almonds

Combine frozen-juice concentrate and water in large pan. Add cloves and cinnamon and bring to a boil. Simmer for 5 minutes. Add raisins and almonds and let sit for 10 minutes. Strain. Reheat and pour into mugs. Spoon a few raisins and almonds (no cloves) into each. About 6 to 8 servings.

Glögg for a Crowd

1 pint bottle cranberry juice   6 whole cloves
1 quart apple cider   2 cinnamon sticks
1 cup raisins   6 or 8 cardamon seeds, cracked
¼ pound candied orange peel   1 small can frozen orange juice
½ cup slivered almonds   2 1-quart bottles ginger ale

Combine everything but orange juice and ginger ale and heat to boiling point. Cool, cover and put in refrigerator overnight. When ready to serve, reheat but do not boil. Add frozen orange juice and ginger ale and heat again.

Spoon a bit of the fruit and nut mixture into each cup. Ladle in the Glögg. This will serve about 35 skiers, one cup each.

Tea Bread

Make at home and bring with you.

1 cup sugar	½ teaspoon baking soda
¼ cup butter	½ teaspoon salt
1 cup All-Bran cereal	1½ cups mashed bananas, mashed
1 egg	with
1½ cups flour	2 tablespoons water
2 teaspoons baking powder	1 teaspoon vanilla

½ cup chopped walnuts

Cream the butter and sugar. Add bran and mix well. Add egg. Mix flour, baking powder, soda and salt together and add to bran mix alternately with the banana and water mixture. Add vanilla and nuts. Let stand in loaf pan for ½ hour before baking for 1 hour at 350° F.

Scottish Scones   (To serve with tea)

3 tablespoons brown sugar	1 cup butter
Powdered sugar	2 cups sifted flour

Put brown sugar into 1-cup measuring cup and fill to top with powdered sugar. Pour into bowl, add butter, and cream well. Add flour. Mix well. Form into 2 rolls about 6 inches long. Wrap in wax paper and put into refrigerator overnight. Slice thin and bake for 10 minutes in 400° F. oven.

Quiche Lorraine   (Serve with tea or Glühwein)

Commit this to memory and make it wherever you are. It's a winner anyplace, anytime.

½ package piecrust mix	2 cups cream
12 slices bacon, fried and crumbled	½ teaspoon salt
	¼ teaspoon pepper
1 cup grated Swiss cheese	¼ teaspoon sugar
1 tablespoon soft butter	Pinch nutmeg
4 eggs	Pinch cayenne

Mix pie dough, roll out, and fit into a 10-inch glass pie plate. Put in refrigerator while you fry bacon. Grate the cheese and set aside.

Fry the bacon. When ready to assemble, spread the piecrust with soft butter, sprinkle with the bacon, then the cheese. Beat eggs lightly in a bowl. Add cream and seasonings. Mix and pour over cheese and bacon.

Bake for 15 minutes at 425° F. then for 15 minutes at 300° F. Test with silver knife. It should come out clean when done. To serve, cut as you would any pie, but make the wedges thin. It can serve up to 10 people because it's so rich.

QUICHE LOUISIANE: Omit bacon and substitute tiny cooked shrimp or large ones cut up. Mix with a little chili sauce and dash of Tabasco.

QUICHE WHATEVER: Omit bacon and substitute chopped cooked ham, tongue, Canadian bacon, cut-up anchovy fillets, whatever.

Salzburger Nockerl   (Serve with Glühwein. Serves 4)

4 eggs, separated   ½ cup sugar
⅛ teaspoon cream of tartar   3 tablespoons flour
⅛ teaspoon salt   ¼ cup butter
                 Vanilla sugar (see below)

Beat egg whites with cream of tartar and salt until foamy. Beat in sugar, 1 tablespoon at a time, until egg whites are shiny. Keep beating until the whites form peaks. Beat yolks with flour until thick and light, then carefully fold into whites. Melt butter in a frying pan until it bubbles. Put the batter in the pan in four mounds and fry until the bottoms are brown (about 2 minutes). Put pan in 325° F. oven for about 7 minutes to brown the tops. Sprinkle with vanilla sugar and serve. One to a person.

Instead of vanilla sugar you can use cinnamon and sugar, finely grated Swiss chocolate or just a dribble of your favorite liqueur.

VANILLA SUGAR: Store 1 cup sifted powdered sugar with 1 split vanilla bean in a tightly covered container for at least 24 hours.

Gâteau Mammoth Mountain   Serve with Glühwein.

Make this at home and bring with you in the car. Or make it the might before you plan to serve it. This is not a last-minute deal. Also makes an excellent canapé.)

2 cups garlic croutons, crushed fine. Measure after you crush them. (To crush, put between pieces of wax paper and roll with a rolling pin.)
¼ cup butter, melted
1 large carton sour cream
1 cup very sharp Cheddar cheese, grated

1 small jar stuffed green olives
1 green pepper, chopped
½ an onion, chopped
2 tablespoons parsley, chopped
½ teaspoon each salt and garlic salt
¼ teaspoon celery seed
¼ teaspoon dry mustard
1 hard-boiled egg, chopped

Blend crumbs and butter and press into the sides and bottom of a 9-inch glass pie pan as you would for a cheesecake crust. Save out about ½ cup crumbs for top. Reserve a few olives for decoration and chop the rest. Blend everything but chopped egg and spread over crumb mixture in pan. Top with the rest of the crumbs mixed with finely chopped hard-boiled egg. Decorate with a few stuffed-olive slices. Chill thoroughly and cut into thin wedges to serve.

Fondue Time

According to tradition, a man is supposed to cook it, but even the Swiss don't care if a woman takes over. The secret of a perfect fondue is in the way you stir it. Tradition, again, dictates big swoops with a wooden spoon in a figure-eight pattern.

If a guest should lose the bread in the pot, the penalty is a kiss. (Tradition used to make you pay for the dinner, but so much for tradition!)

It is made in an earthenware fondue pot, over an alcohol burner. If you don't have a fondue pot, make in a double boiler and transfer to a casserole with a candle warmer.

Fondue

1 clove garlic, peeled and halved
1¼ cups sauterne (good brand)
¾ pound natural Swiss cheese cut julienne (about 3 cups)

1 tablespoon best flour
Dash freshly ground pepper
Dash nutmeg
3 tablespoons Kirsch

French rolls or French bread cut into bite-size pieces with crust on at least one side

ᴧᴧᴧ

Rub the inside of fondue pot with the cut surface of garlic. Pour in sauterne and warm until air bubbles start to rise. Don't cover and *don't boil*. Remember to stir all the time from now on. Add a handful of cheese, which you have tossed with the flour. Wait until cheese has melted before tossing in another handful. But keep stirring, lady; keep stirring.

After all the cheese is in, stir in seasoning and Kirsch. Now . . . dunk! If fondue becomes too thick, pour in a little warmed sauterne. This will serve 8 if you limit them by saying that dinner follows.

NOTE: Kirsch is traditional. Don't fret about it's cost because it has many uses. It's delicious spooned over fresh fruit and it is perfect for Cherries Jubilee or Crêpes Suzette as it burns better than brandy.

Baked French Fondue   (Serves 6 to 10, depending)

1 long loaf French bread	5 cups hot milk
½ cup butter	1½ teaspoons Worcestershire
½ cup sharp mustard [stone ground or with horseradish]	sauce
	1 teaspoon seasoned salt
1½ pounds Cheddar cheese, sliced thin	⅛ teaspoon cayenne
	⅛ teaspoon paprika
4 eggs, well beaten	

Slice bread and spread with mixture of butter and mustard. Then cut into cubes and put into large greased casserole, alternately with slices of cheese. Combine everything else and pour over the cheese and bread. Put into refrigerator overnight. Bake, uncovered, in 350° F. oven for 1½ hours. Serve as hors d'oeuvres on dessert plates, with forks.

EMERGENCY FONDUE: Add a quarter can of white wine to a can of cheese soup. Heat in fondue pot and serve surrounded with bread cubes. Add a couple of tablespoons of Kirsch if you have it. If you don't have fondue forks for spearing bread, serve hot French-fried potatoes. Use fingers to dip potatoes into cheese. (Frozen french fries cooked in the oven work fine.)

BEEF FONDUE: Beef Fondue (Fondue Bourguignon) is a complete meal, so that's what our first dinner menu will feature.

Ski Dinner for Eight

BEEF FONDUE
SAUCES
BAKED POTATOES
TOSSED SALAD
FRENCH ROLLS
BRANDIED FRUIT

TO SERVE:

Bertolini, Chianti (Italian)

or

Almadén, Gewürztraminer (California)

or

Paul Masson, Rubion (California)

BEEF FONDUE: Instead of dipping bread in hot cheese, each diner fries pieces of beef fillet in hot oil and then dips them in a variety of sauces. Each participant is given a plate of bite-size beef cubes, a fondue fork and access to the several sauces. In the middle of the table place a large metal pot of hot oil over an alcohol burner. I usually use my old Dutch oven.

Rub pot with a garlic clove, peeled and halved. Pour into it about ½ pint peanut oil and ½ pound butter. Heat to the boiling point and keep at this temperature. Each guest puts 2 or 3 meat cubes in at a time and cooks to desired doneness. Allow the equivalent of one beef fillet, 1 inch thick, per person.

Mushroom Sauce

1 can mushroom soup
1 small can mushroom pieces
Few drops lemon juice

Seasoned salt and pepper
1 small onion chopped and fried in a little butter

Put all together and heat. Serve hot.

Wine Sauce

1 can wine soup (gourmet section of market)

½ cup port
1 tablespoon chili sauce

Mix and serve hot.

Pink Sauce

To ⅔ cup mayonnaise add ⅓ cup chili sauce and a few drops lemon juice. Mix and serve cold.

Mexican Sauce

Heat a can of XLNT Enchilada Sauce (or bottled Taco Sauce) and serve hot.

Tartar Sauce

⅓ cup sweet pickle relish
1 cup mayonnaise

½ onion, grated or chopped fine
1 tablespoon capers

Mix and serve cold.

Baked Potatoes

One for each person. Scrub, cut an X in the top of each. Rub with bacon grease. Bake at 400° F. for 40 to 45 minutes. To serve, squeeze and they pop open at the X. Let each person spoon on one of the beef sauces.

Brandied Fruit   (Serves 8)

1 large can Bing cherries, pitted
1 large can apricot halves
1 large can Freestone peach halves

1 lemon, juice and grated rind
1 orange, juice and grated rind
1 cup brown sugar

2 tablespoons brandy

Drain all fruit and save juice. Arrange all the fruit in a Pyrex baking dish. Add grated rinds and saved juices. Sprinkle brown sugar evenly over top of fruit. Heat thoroughly in a 300° F. oven until sugar melts. Add brandy. Serve hot or cold, with a side dish of sour cream.

NOTE: You can actually use any canned fruit you find on the shelf. In an emergency I have made this with three cans of fruit and a shot glass of brandy.

Light Supper Aprés Fondue   (Serves 4)

FRENCH ONION SOUP
CREAMED SPINACH SALAD SUPREME
FRENCH BREAD
DESSERT VAIL
COFFEE

TO SERVE:

Souverain, Johannesberg Riesling (California)
or
Wente Brothers, Pinot Blanc (California)
or
Italian Swiss Colony, Chablis (California)

French Onion Soup

3 cans beef bouillon
1 tablespoon melted butter
2 large onions, thinly sliced
1 teaspoon salt
¼ teaspoon pepper
Loaf French bread
1 pound Swiss cheese, sliced

In the morning before you leave for the slopes, heat bouillon. In a frying pan, melt butter and sauté onions until good and brown. Add them to the bouillon with the seasonings and refrigerate until dinnertime. Cut the bread in slices and toast. Leave it on a plate on drainboard.

Just before serving, reheat bouillon. Cut cheese into small pieces. Into a large casserole pour all but one cup of soup and sprinkle ½ cup cheese on top. Arrange a layer of toasted bread slices on soup and sprinkle with half of the remaining cheese, then the rest of the bread and the rest of the cheese. Pour the last bit of soup over all. Place in a hot (475° F.) oven 5 to 7 minutes until cheese is melted and bubbly.

Creamed Spinach Salad Supreme   (Serves 4)

2 bunches fresh spinach leaves (the smaller the leaves the better)
⅔ cup mayonnaise
⅔ cup sour cream
8 anchovies, mashed
2 tablespoons chopped green-onion tops
2 tablespoons chopped parsley
2 tablespoons vinegar
2 tablespoons lemon juice
2 cloves garlic, crushed
½ cup Dixie-Fry croutons (or other packaged croutons or use cubes of cheese)

Wash and dry spinach. Mix rest of ingredients except croutons, and lightly toss with spinach leaves. Add croutons (or cheese) just before putting on chilled salad plates.

Dessert, Vail   (Serves 8)

1 angel-food cake   1 pint sour cream
1½ cups dry sauterne   Apricot halves, canned or frozen
                     Cinnamon

Cut cake horizontally in half, making two rings. Place rings side
by side on a platter and dribble the wine slowly over them until it is
all absorbed. Frost both halves of the cake with sour cream, decorate
with apricots and sprinkle with cinnamon.

Family Style Ski Dinner for Eight

BEEF BUENO

ANTIPASTO PLATTER

TAO CAKES

COFFEE

TO SERVE:

Valpolicella (Italian)

or

Louis Martini, Mt. Zinfandel (California)

or

Gallo, Hearty Burgundy (California)

Beef Bueno   (Serves 8)

½ cup flour (more if necessary)   ¼ cup brandy
Seasoned salt   1 pound fresh mushrooms, sliced
Pepper   1 7-ounce can green chili salsa
 4 pounds top round steak, cubed   1 cup consommé
 ¼ cup olive oil (to begin)   1 tablespoon wine vinegar
 5 tablespoons butter   ¼ teaspoon marjoram
 4 cloves unpeeled garlic (Just   ¼ cup chopped parsley
   take my word for it.)   1 package refrigerator biscuits

This may be prepared in the morning. Put flour, salt and pepper in
a brown paper bag and shake the meat cubes in the mixture until
coated. In Dutch oven, heat oil and 3 tablespoons of the butter with
the garlic cloves. Brown the meat well. Add more oil if necessary. Before

removing from pan, pour brandy over and ignite. Toss out the garlic and put meat in heat-proof dish.

Add to Dutch oven the other 2 tablespoons butter and brown the mushrooms. Then add the salsa. Add the meat to the mushrooms and add consommé, vinegar, marjoram, parsley. Cover, simmer 1½ hours.

At night, when ready to serve, pour into a serving casserole, top with biscuits (see below) and bake in 400° F. oven for 10 to 15 minutes. If you refrigerate the meat and sauce, heat it for about ½ hour before you top with biscuits.

Biscuits

Separate 1 package of refrigerator biscuits, dip in melted butter and then in Parmesan cheese. Arrange on top of beef.

Antipasto Platter

On a platter arrange lettuce leaves, strips of pimento, ripe olives, anchovies, celery sticks, sliced tomatoes, garlic salami, pieces of monterey jack or Swiss cheese. Pour over all a vinegar-and-oil dressing, sprinkle with capers, salt and freshly ground pepper.

Tao Cakes

6 eggs, separated	6 tablespoons flour
6 tablespoons sugar	Grated rind of 1 lemon
½ cup vegetable oil	

Whip yolks, add sugar and mix thoroughly. Sift in flour and mix well. Beat whites stiff and fold in. Add rind. In a small skillet heat vegetable oil as you would for doughnuts and fry batter, a tablespoonful at a time, until golden brown. Drain on paper. These cakes can be kept for a week in a tight lidded jar. When ready to serve, mix in a pan:

White wine (about 2 cups)	1 stick cinnamon
½ lemon, sliced thin	

This is the perfect dessert after a big dinner. You can wait awhile and then serve cakes from a chafing dish in the living room in front of the fire. Drop the cakes into the pan and bring to a boil. Simmer slowly for ½ hour. Serve hot.

VIII

If Your Man Shoots

If it flies, runs, walks or sneaks up on you from behind, your sportsman may have just the right gun and just the right shot to bring it home for dinner.

So, I suggest to you: know your adversary: the game—and also know your man!

Starting with game that flies:

PIGEON

Invite one person for each pigeon. Dinner parties featuring birds must be planned this way. An alternative suggestion: have a couple of frozen Cornish game hens ready to fill in. Some men demand that their birds be cooked to feature their unadulterated particular taste, (the bird's, that is). Others shoot more for the comradeship and just as soon have you apply the gourmet touch to whatever they bring in. But, as your sportsman will tell you, it is absolutely *de rigueur* to eat what you shoot. So, as cook, it's best to know what you're doing.

Pigeon Party for Six

PLAIN PIGEON ON BIRD TOAST
RICE LA COSTA
CUCUMBERS GARONNE
HONEY CUSTARD
COFFEE

TO SERVE:

Franken, Reisling in Flask Bottle (German)
  or
Inglenook, Pinot Chardonnay (California)
  or
Gallo, Rhine Garten (California)

Plain Pigeon

Rinse birds and pat dry. Snip off wing tips with poultry shears. Shake in paper bag with flour, seasoned salt and pepper. Fry in hot bacon grease until crisp and brown but still pink and juicy inside. You test for doneness with a fork. Serve on Bird Toast.

BIRD TOAST: Cut slices of bread 1½ inches thick from a loaf of stale white bread. Remove crusts. With small sawtooth knife, like a grapefruit knife, hollow out a piece of the middle, but don't go all the way through. Fry in butter until golden brown. Drain. Serve each bird on a separate piece. Decorate with parsley or watercress.

Rice la Costa   (Serves 6 generously)

1 package frozen spinach
1 pound cheddar or sharp American cheese grated
1 cup milk
4 eggs
3 cups cooked rice
¼ cup butter, melted
2 teaspoons salt
1 tablespoon A-1 or Worcestershire Sauce
½ small onion, chopped fine
Pinch basil, thyme and oregano

Cook and drain spinach. Add everything else, stir, and pack into a casserole. Set in pan of hot water and bake 40 minutes at 350° F.

Cucumbers Garonne   (Serves 6)

3 cucumbers
Salt
Large carton sour cream
½ cup chopped almonds
¼ cup chopped chives (fresh or frozen)
1 tablespoon lemon juice
Ground black pepper

Peel and slice cucumbers paper thin. Sprinkle with salt and let stand for at least 1 hour. Drain off liquid then add other ingredients, mix well.

Honey Custard   (Serves 6)

2½ cups milk   ½ cup honey
  4 eggs, slightly beaten   1 teaspoon vanilla
                    ½ teaspoon cinnamon

Heat milk to scalding. Blend eggs with honey; gradually stir in milk.
Add vanilla and cinnamon, stirring until blended. Pour into 6 custard
cups. Put cups in a pan of hot water and bake in a moderate oven
(350° F.) for 30 minutes or until silver knife, inserted, comes out
clean. Serve in the cups.

Another Menu Featuring Pigeon

PIGEON KOWLOON
CHINESE SNOW PEAS
MOLDED ORANGE SALAD
HOT ROLLS
STRAWBERRY PIE

TO SERVE:

Mateus, Rosé (French) or
Louis Martini, Mt. Folle Blanche (California) or
Umeshu [Japanese Plum Wine]

(It's often fun to serve a wine that will be a complete surprise to
everyone. Don't be afraid to experiment. This is how you earn your
reputation as a gourmet hostess.)

Pigeon Kowloon

4 pigeons (For more birds, adjust   ½ cup water chestnuts, chopped
  recipe accordingly.)   ¼ cup chopped peanuts
¾ tablespoon bacon grease   ¼ pound fresh mushrooms,
2 cups uncooked rice   chopped
2 stalks celery, chopped   Salt
½ onion, chopped   Pepper
                    Currant jelly

Cut pigeons with duck shears. (You can't prepare anything wild without a pair.) Remove neck and wing tips. If giblets were saved, add them,

with neck and wing tips to a large saucepan filled with at least 4 cups of water, a bay leaf and a couple of peppercorns. Boil gently for stock as you would if cooking turkey.

Melt grease in heavy iron skillet and add the rice. Stir until rice is nice and brown. You may have to add a bit more grease. Take ⅔ cup of the browned rice and ⅔ cup of stock and simmer until rice is cooked. Mix with the celery, onion, nuts and mushrooms and use to stuff birds. Put stuffed birds into a Dutch oven. Dump remaining rice over birds, pour about three cups boiling stock over all and bake, covered, at 350° F. about 1½ hours, or until pigeons are fork tender.

Take pigeons out, put on flat pan, rub butter and a little dab of currant jelly over them and stick under broiler to brown. Split pigeons lengthwise and serve on rice.

Chinese Snow Peas

These are the dainty new peas that you eat, pods and all. Wash them. Pick off the ends and string as you would a bean. Boil for 2 to 5 minutes in enough water to barely cover. Add salt, pepper and a dab of butter. Figure on a handful of pods per person. (You can also buy them frozen.)

Molded Orange Salad   (Serves 6)

1 cup fresh orange juice
1 package orange Jello
1 cup buttermilk

¼ cup chopped nuts
3 large oranges, peeled and sliced
½ cup seedless grapes, cut in half

Heat the juice until it simmers. Remove from heat and stir in the Jello until it is completely dissolved. Stir in the buttermilk. Chill until mixture begins to set, then add nuts and grapes. Chill until firm.

To serve, take six plates and arrange a couple of leaves of lettuce, slices of orange and a scoop of the mold on each. Pass a bowl of vinegar and oil dressing.

Strawberry Pie with Butter-Crunch Crust

CRUST:

½ cup butter
¼ cup brown sugar

1 cup sifted flour
½ cup pecans, chopped

Make crust first. Heat oven to 400° F. Mix ingredients with hands. Spread in oblong pan and bake for 15 minutes. Take from oven and immediately press mixture against bottom and sides of pie pan. While it is cooling, prepare filling.

FILLING:

1 pint of berries, sliced   1 pint of berries, whole

Line piecrust with whole berries, sprinkle lightly with powdered sugar. Cook sliced berries with

1 cup sugar   3 tablespoons cornstarch

for 20 minutes. Add 2 tablespoons lemon juice and cook a little longer. Cool, pour over whole berries to fill pie shell. Cool until ready to serve.

DOVES

Doves being smaller than pigeons, allow at least two per person. If your man has the soul of a true hunter, he will want to taste the meat, so keep his doves pink and juicy. The best way I've found to accomplish this is just to panfry them as you do the pigeon. Or try this:

Doves Claret for Four

DOVES CLARET
SPAGHETTI WITH FRESH PARSLEY
SPINACH SALAD WITH AVOCADO DRESSING
PLATTER OF FRESH FRUIT
COFFEE

TO SERVE:

Italian Swiss Colony, Claret (California)
or
Louis Martini, Mt. Zinfandel (California)
or
Inglenook, Cabernet Sauvignon (California)

Doves Claret   (Serves 4)

8 doves
4 tablespoons flour with salt and
  pepper

¼ cup olive oil
¼ cup butter
2 cloves garlic
1 cup claret wine

Rinse doves and pat dry. Snip off wing tips with poultry shears. Shake doves in paper bag with flour and seasonings. In iron skillet heat oil, butter and peeled garlic. When hot, brown the doves. Remove the garlic, turn down fire and pour wine into pan. Add some water to bring liquid up to cover the doves ¾ of the way. Simmer for about 1½ hours. To test for tenderness, prick leg with fork. Place birds on top of platter of spaghetti. Thicken gravy with flour left in sack. Pour over doves.

Spaghetti with Fresh Parsley   (Serves 4 to 6)

¼ cup butter
1 tablespoon olive oil
1 small onion, chopped
⅔ cup chopped fresh parsley
½ teaspoon nutmeg

¼ teaspoon salt
¼ teaspoon pepper
1 package (8 ounces) spaghetti
2 tablespoons grated Parmesan
  cheese

While doves cook, make sauce. Melt butter, add olive oil and sauté the onion until it becomes translucent. Add parsley, nutmeg, salt and pepper. 15 minutes before doves are ready, cook spaghetti in boiling salted water as directed on package. Drain. Place on heat-proof platter, pour sauce over, sprinkle with cheese and put in oven for 5 minutes before you put the doves on top. It all makes a neat mixed-up flavor.

Spinach Salad with Avocado Dressing

3 to 4 bunches nice fresh spinach, washed, dried and cut up. Use only the smaller inside leaves.

DRESSING:

2 avocados, mashed
3 tablespoons white wine
Juice of ½ lemon (more if you like)

Seasoned salt and pepper
¼ pound bacon, cooked, to crumble over top of salad

Mix everything but bacon in bowl. Pour over spinach. Add bacon and serve immediately.

PARTRIDGE

Quail and partridge recipes are interchangeable. Also recipes for Cornish game hens. You can do anything to a partridge you would do to a small chicken. (Although I can't imagine shooting a small chicken. However. . . .)

Partridge Buffet for Six

ROAST PARTRIDGE
GRILLED APPLE SLICES
ONION SOUFFLÉ
MELON WITH KIRSCH
PLATTER OF BEST COOKIES

TO SERVE:

Les Caillerets, Volnay (French)
    or
Christian Brothers, Sauvignon Blanc (California)
    or
Almadén, Chablis (California)

Roast Partridge   (1 per person)

Truss birds. Salt and pepper inside cavities. Rub breasts generously with butter. (The birds'!) Place in hot oven (425° F.) for 45 minutes. Baste at least every 10 minutes. Put birds on a platter. To drippings in pan add juice of 1 lemon, 1 tablespoon Worcestershire sauce, and 1 teaspoon dry mustard. Heat on top of stove and pour over birds. Place on platter and surround with grilled apple slices.

Grilled Apple Slices   (Serves 6)

3 large apples   ¼ cup sugar
3 tablespoons butter   ¼ cup muscatel wine

Pare and core apples and cut into thin slices. Place in skillet with butter, sprinkle with sugar, cover and sauté over moderate heat for about 5 minutes. Turn apples once or twice. Add wine, cover again and simmer until tender.

Onion Soufflé (Serves 6)

5 tablespoons butter
1 large onion, chopped
1 clove garlic, crushed
4 tablespoons flour

1 teaspoon seasoned salt
1 teaspoon seasoned pepper
¼ teaspoon nutmeg
1 cup milk

9 eggs, separated

Melt butter in a pan. Add onion and garlic and cook until onion is light brown. Add flour and seasonings and stir with a wire whisk until smooth. When sauce bubbles, remove from heat and stir in milk. Cook again until mixture is thick. Cool and beat in yolks. Heat again. Whip the whites until firm peaks form. When sauce has cooled again, fold in whites, ½ at a time. Pour into soufflé dish and bake in 375° F. oven for 40 minutes (or 20 minutes if you make individual soufflés).

Melon with Kirsch (Serves 6)

2 cantaloupes (or other similar melons)
1 box strawberries [1 cup]
1 box raspberries or blackberries [1 cup]

1 cup seedless grapes
1 can pineapple tidbits
¼ cup sugar
1 tablespoon Kirsch

In morning cut off piece from one end of each melon to make 4- or 5-inch round opening. Clean and hull berries. With spoon, scoop out seeds. With a ball scoop, take out melon meat. Mix the mellon balls with berries, pineapple and grapes. Pour over sugar and Kirsch. Put fruit into melon cavities, replace tops and refrigerate until ready to serve. Put "as is" on buffet table and let guests help themselves.

Partridge Dinner for Four

PARTRIDGE IN CREAM
HERBED RICE
GREEN BEANS IN ARTICHOKE BOTTOMS
GRASSHOPPER PIE
COFFEE

TO SERVE:

Gevrey-Chambertin (French) or
Clos des Ducs, Volnay (French) or
Almadén, Dry Semillon Sauterne (California)

Partridge in Cream   (Serves 4)

4 partridge
1 stick butter
4 small green onions, chopped with tops

½ can consommé
3 shot glasses brandy
Small carton sour cream

Truss birds as for roasting. In a heavy Dutch oven heat the butter. Add onions and the birds and fry until all are golden brown. (Always turn birds with two wooden spoons so you don't prick the skin.) Add ½ can consommé, the brandy and sour cream. Put cover on pot and bake in 350° F. oven for about 30 minutes or until tender. Serve over rice. (Cornish game hens may be substituted.)

Herbed Rice   (Serves 6)

2 onions, chopped
1 clove garlic, crushed
3 tablespoons butter
1 cup raw rice
3 cups chicken broth (or 3 cubes chicken bouillon dissolved in 3 cups hot water)

1 teaspoon marjoram
1 teaspoon chervil
1 tablespoon chopped parsley
1 teaspoon thyme

Cook onion and garlic in butter until tender. Add the rice and brown slightly, stirring constantly. Add broth and herbs. Bring to a boil, reduce heat, cover and cook until rice is tender and liquid is absorbed (about 20 minutes).

Green Beans in Artichoke Bottoms   (Serves 4 to 6)

1 can green beans, cut
1 cup oil-and-vinegar dressing (bottled okay)
4 green onions, chopped, including tops

6 anchovies, chopped
Canned or frozen artichoke bottoms
2 tablespoons capers

(This is the salad *and* the vegetable.)

Drain beans and soak in ½ cup of dressing with the onion and anchovies for an hour. Add basil to remaining ½ cup dressing and soak the artichokes in it. To assemble, arrange a leaf of lettuce on salad plate, add bottom of artichoke and spoonful of beans. Put the two dressings together, add capers and pour over all

Grasshopper Pie   (Serves 6 to 8)

20 chocolate wafers, crushed	2 ounces white crème de cocao
¼ cup melted butter	2 ounces green crème de menthe
½ pound marshmallows	½ pint cream, heavy
1 cup milk	1 bar semi-sweet chocolate

Mix the crushed wafers and melted butter together and pat into 9-inch pie plate for crust.

Melt the marshmallows with milk in top of double boiler. Cool and carefully fold in the two liqueurs. Whip cream until firm and fold into marshmallow mixture. Pour into crust. Shave chocolate over top and refrigerate for several hours.

TO SERVE WITH GRASSHOPPER PIE:

Crème de menthe over ice

DUCKS

Ducks, truly, should be eaten medium rare to blood rare. Don't analyze it or dwell on it—just do it. Here's a chart from a charming older man who shot and cooked duck for sixty years:

Small duck (teal, widgeon, etc.); 20 minutes, 5 minutes at 555° F., 15 minutes at 450° F.

Mallard; 30 minutes, 5 minutes at 550° F., 25 minutes at 450° F.

Brant; 45 minutes, 5 minutes at 550° F., 40 minutes at 450° F.

Duck for Six

ROAST DUCK WITH SAUCE ROHNER

WILD RICE

AVOCADO ASPIC

CRISP CARAMEL CUSTARD

COFFEE

TO SERVE:

Inglenook, Pinot Chardonnay (California)
  or
Chateau Figeac, St.-Émilion (French)
André, Sparkling Burgundy (California)

Roast Duck

Allow one duck per person. Men often eat two and somtimes three, but I prefer to share and just serve one per person. Stuff the cavity of each duck with 2 or 3 pieces of celery and 1 big piece of onion. (This is to draw out any fishy taste. Throw away stuffing after baking.)

Put ducks, breast side up, in flat baking pan. Lay strips of bacon over breasts. Baste 2 or 3 times during cooking. Test for doneness by making tiny incisions next to breast bone. It will look rarer than it actually is, so be prepared.

Sauce Rohner   (For 3 ducks)

This alone is worth the price of the book. Put a metal pie tin that you don't ever intend to use again on top of stove burner. Heat really hot. Pour 3 teaspoons Worcestershire sauce in pan and stand back. It beads, burns, smokes, spits and dilates your nostrils. Turn off heat, add another teapoon Worcestershire. This will just boil. Stir it with burnt Worcestershire, mixing well. Then add:

½ stick butter, melted   2 more teaspoons Worcestershire
Juice of 1 big lemon   sauce
                  2 teaspoons paprika

Turn on heat and boil, gently for 2 or 3 minutes, stirring constantly. Serve in bowl with ladle.

Better quadruple the amounts. Just writing about it makes my mouth water. Everyone I've ever talked to who has cooked duck has a favorite sauce. I think Sauce Rohner is the best, but here are a couple of good alternatives:

Sauce Menlo

½ cup Burgundy   1 teaspoon Worcestershire sauce
½ cup orange juice   1 clove garlic, cut up
½ cup currant jelly   Juice of 1 lemon

Mix all together, simmer for 1 hour, and remove from heat. Just before serving add 1 stick butter and heat just until butter melts.

Cumberland Duck Sauce

⅓ cup orange juice
Grated rind of 1 orange
¼ cup lemon juice
Grated rind of 1 lemon

1 cup powdered sugar
2 tablespoons currant jelly
1 tablespoon grated horseradish

Mix all together, beat well, heat and serve.

Wild Rice with Mushrooms   (Serves 6)

1 stick butter
1 cup wild rice
1 package sliced almonds

½ a green pepper, chopped
½ pound fresh mushrooms, sliced
3 cups chicken broth

Put everything except broth into heavy skillet. Cook and stir until rice turns yellow. Put into casserole with broth, cover tightly and bake in oven at 325° F. for 1 hour. If you have only one oven, bake this first and leave covered on back of stove. Then roast ducks.

Avocado Aspic

1 envelope plain gelatin
½ cup cold water
1 cup unsweetened grapefruit
   juice
2 extra-ripe avocados, mashed

1 teaspoon Worcestershire sauce
½ teaspoon Tabasco Sauce
2 tablespoons minced onion
½ teaspoon seasoned salt
½ cup mayonnaise

Soften gelatin in cold water, then dissolve over hot water. Add grapefruit juice and chill until barely set. Add rest of ingredients, beat with a rotary beater until smooth and pour into ring mold. Chill until firm. Fill center with cherry tomatoes.

Caramel Crisp Custard   (Serves 6)

½ cup brown sugar, firmly packed
½ cup cornflakes
3 eggs, slightly beaten

¼ cup granulated sugar
⅛ teaspoon salt
2 cups scalded milk

1 teaspoon vanilla

Mix together brown sugar and cornflakes. Divide evenly in bottom of 6 buttered custard cups. Combine all remaining ingredients and pour gently into custard cups. Place in pan of hot water and bake in a moderately slow oven, 325° F., for 40 minutes or until a silver knife inserted in center of custard comes out clean. Cool. Turn cups upside down on serving dishes and let stand a minute before removing cup from dish. This allows topping to settle down on custard.

PHEASANT

Unfortunately, pheasant has a tendency to be dry. So when serving roasted, plan to serve a sauce.

> 1 pheasant, cut up, will serve 6
> 1 pheasant, quartered, will serve 4
> 2 pheasants roasted will serve 4
> 1 small pheasant can be eaten by 1 person (or more)
> 2 pheasants are called a brace

Roast Pheasant with Raisin Sauce

Wash birds inside and out. Dry, then salt and pepper the cavities. Inside put celery, apple and onion, cut into pieces. Place birds on a rack in roasting pan. Put bacon over the breasts and roast in 350° F. oven for 1½ to 2 hours. Test as you would a chicken for doneness. During last half hour remove bacon and baste birds with sauce.

Raisin Sauce   (Or use any duck sauce, pages 95, 96)

1 onion, chopped	½ cup dark brown sugar
½ cup seedless raisins	2 tablespoons Worcestershire
1 cup chili sauce	sauce
½ cup water	1 cup sherry

Heat all together. Spooned over pheasant, it mixes with pan juices and is great.

Pineapple Pheasant for Four

PINEAPPLE PHEASANT
SOUFFLÉ POTATOES
SWISS SALAD
MOORISH ORANGES

TO SERVE:

Paul Masson, Emerald Day (California)

or

Château Cos d'Estournel (French)

or

Charles Krug, Johannesberg Riesling (California)

Pheasant Pineapple   (Serves 4)

1 pheasant, quartered	1 teaspoon finely chopped parsley
½ stick soft butter	Juice of ½ lemon
½ teaspoon dry mustard	4 slices ham, very thin slices
½ teaspoon salt	1 cup white wine
1 teaspoon curry powder	½ fresh pineapple, sliced
1 teaspoon paprika	or 1 small can pineapple rings

Mix together everything but pheasant, ham, wine and pineapple. Rub this over the pieces of bird. Use all of it. In Dutch oven place slices of pineapple. Put the pieces of bird on pineapple and put a thin *thin* slice of ham over each piece. Mix ½ cup wine with ½ cup water (or pineapple juice), pour over pheasant, cover and bake in hot 450° F. oven for 30 minutes. Uncover and bake 20 to 30 minutes more, or until brown.

Remove pheasant, test for doneness as you would chicken, pour sauce, including pineapple, into blender and whir until liquid. Add ½ cup wine and reheat. Pour over bird. Excellent!

Soufflé Potatoes

These are not hard to make, although when you see them in a restaurant you might think so. Allow 1½ potatoes per person. Peel the potatoes and cut lengthwise in slices about ¼ inch thick. As you slice them, dump into ice water. Soak for at least 30 minutes.

In electric fryer, or deep-fat fryer, heat 2 cups cooking oil to 250° F. and fry potatoes until they rise to the surface. This takes about 5 minutes. Remove and drain on paper towel. Cool until they are cold. If you are in a hurry, put them in the refrigerator.

Heat grease to 425° F. and drop in the cold potatoes. Remove them

when puffed and brown. Sprinkle with salt and pepper and serve hot.
If some of the potatoes refuse to puff, cool and fry again.

Swiss Salad   (Serves 4)

½ pound coarse grated Swiss cheese
1 cup cooked, frozen, or canned green beans, *not* French cut
1 cup diced celery

1 cup chopped parsley tops
1 small head butter lettuce
1 small head red lettuce or romaine
Oil-and-vinegar dressing

Tear lettuce into bite-size pieces. Mix all ingredients except dressing.
Add dressing and mix again.

Moorish Oranges   (Serves 4 to 6)

4 navel oranges
1 tablespoon sugar
¼ cup dates, cut up

¼ cup dried figs, cut up
¼ cup almonds, slivered
2 jiggers curaçao or Cointreau

Peel and slice the oranges very thin. Arrange in an overlapping layer
on a glass plate. Sprinkle the sugar, dates, figs and nuts over oranges
and pour on the liqueur. Chill well before serving. If it doesn't look
moist enough, add ½ cup orange juice. Serve with a few lady fingers.

BIG GAME

Venison is the meat of deer, elk or moose. The recipes are interchangeable. Of bear, you eat ham steaks and saddle, of boar you eat ham, chops and sides (made into bacon), and of wild bighorn sheep (in states where not protected) you eat leg, loin and chops.

Big game should be cut up by an expert. You should be told, however, which end and what parts you will be given to cook.

Practically everything belonging to a deer is edible. When cooking a saddle (whole loin) or haunch (whole hind leg), you may want to marinate it first. You *must* if it's an older animal, and *always* marinate elk and moose.

vv

Classic Marinade for All Big Game

1 bottle Gallo Hearty Burgundy	2 cloves garlic, sliced
1 cup vinegar	1 carrot, chopped
1 cup water	3 stalks celery and tops, chopped
2 bay leaves	Coarsely ground pepper
1 teaspoon thyme	Salt
2 onions, sliced	A few juniper berries

Big cuts should soak for 2 to 4 days, smaller cuts for 24 hours. Turn once in a while. Keep cool and cover crock or pan with foil.

Big Game Menu I

ROAST SADDLE OF VENISON

SAUCE ST. HUBERT

RICE VALENCIA

SALAD MACÉDOINE

ANGEL CUSTARD CAKE

TO SERVE:

Beaulieu Vineyard, Pinot Noir (California)
or
Jadot, Côte de Beaune-Villages (French)
or
Gallo, Hearty Burgundy (California)

Roast Saddle of Venison

Trim off all fat. Soak saddle in marinade. When ready to cook, dry thoroughly and put into roasting pan. Put slices of salt pork or bacon on top of meat. Put a little oil in pan and stick into very hot oven (450° F.) for 30 minutes. Reduce heat to 350° F., pour in a cup of marinade and roast, uncovered, for about 1½ hours. Add more marinade as needed. For rare, plan on 10 to 15 minutes per pound; well done 20 to 25 minutes per pound, starting from room temperature. To be very accurate use a meat thermometer. Serve with Cumberland Sauce (*see* duck section, p. 94) or with St. Hubert Sauce. (St. Hubert is the patron saint of hunters and fishermen.)

St. Hubert Sauce

½ pound fresh mushrooms, chopped
2 chopped green onions
¼ cup butter

1 tablespoon parsley, chopped
½ cup white wine
½ cup marinade
1 tablespoon tomato sauce

2 tablespoons brandy

Fry the mushrooms and onions in butter. Add rest of ingredients and simmer for a few minutes.

Rice Valencia   (Serves 6 to 8)

3 tablespoons good olive oil
1 green pepper, chopped
1 medium onion, chopped
1 cup rice
3 cups liquid (bouillon cubes in water, consommé, or chicken broth, all okay)

3 tablespoons tomato paste
3 Spanish sweet peppers, cut up (canned okay)
½ cup cooked fresh peas (or canned petit pois)
¼ teaspoon saffron
1 teaspoon salt

1 teaspoon pepper

Heat oil in skillet with lid. Cook the green pepper and onion. Add the rest of the ingredients, cover, and cook over low heat until all liquid is absorbed. About 25 to 35 minutes.

Salad Macédoine

1 bunch watercress
2 kinds lettuce
2 oranges, peeled and sectioned

2 unpeeled apples, diced
½ cup good sharp cheese, cubed
French dressing

Cut watercress, tear lettuce and put in salad bowl. Add oranges, apples and cheese. Pour over French dressing and mix all together.

Angel Custard Cake

Divide an angel-food cake into 3 horizontal layers

CUSTARD:

1 tablespoon unflavored gelatin
¼ cup water
1 pint whipping cream

4 egg yolks
1 cup powdered sugar
1 teaspoon vanilla

Put gelatin in ¼ cup cold water and dissolve in pan set in another pan of hot water. Whip cream and beat the egg yolks. Add sugar and vanilla. Mix with gelatin and spread between the layers and on top of cake. Chill in refrigerator for about 10 hours.

Big Game Menu II

VENISON GOULASH PIEDMONT

THIN NOODLES

HUNT CLUB SALAD

MELONS MELBA

TO SERVE:

Beringer Bros., Barenblut (California)

or

Chambertin-Clos de Bèze (French)

or

Paul Masson, Gamay Beaujolais (California)

Venison Goulash Piedmont   (Serves 8 to 10)

2 pounds venison, cut in cubes
½ teaspoon seasoned salt
½ teaspoon paprika
2 tablespoons flour
2 tablespoons butter
2 carrots, sliced
1 onion, sliced
1 cup Gallo, Hearty Burgundy

1 beef bouillon cube dissolved in
1 cup hot water
2 tablespoons tomato paste
1 bay leaf
½ teaspoon thyme
2 potatoes, cubed
½ pound fresh mushrooms, clean and whole

1 can tiny white onions

Shake the venison in seasoned flour in a paper bag. Cook in hot butter until golden brown. Add carrots and sliced onion. Simmer until onions start to turn brown. Add wine, bouillon, tomato paste and seasonings. Bring to boil and add potatoes. Bake covered in 425° F. oven for 30 minutes. Add mushrooms and white onions. Cook for 10 minutes more. Remove bay leaf and skim off fat. Thicken with flour and water if sauce seems too thin. Serve over noodles or make a Hunter's Pie.

Hunter's Pie I: (Use for any stew, goulash, or ragout.)

Prepare 1 package piecrust mix, roll out ⅔ of it and fit into deep-dish casserole. Pour goulash, thickened, onto bottom crust. Roll out rest of dough. Cut out pieces with a cookie cutter shaped like a reindeer and place on top of goulash. Bake in 400° F. oven until top browns. (About 15 minutes.)

Hunter's Pie II

Pour thickened goulash into pan, warm.

Take can of refrigerator biscuits, dip in melted butter, then in grated Parmesan cheese. Put on top of goulash, return to 425° F. oven, for 10 minutes or until biscuits brown.

Hunt Club Salad   (Serves 8)

6 strips bacon
4 tablespoons cider vinegar
4 teaspoons sugar

Seasoned salt
Seasoned pepper
2 heads romaine lettuce

2 hard-boiled eggs, chopped

Cook bacon until crisp. Remove to paper to drain. Add vinegar, sugar, salt and pepper to the grease left from bacon. Bring to a boil. Turn the washed and dried heads of romaine on side and with a sharp knife cut in ¼- to ½-inch slices. Dump lettuce into a wooden bowl and pour the hot dressing over. Drop in bacon, crumbled, and mix. Top with chopped hard-boiled eggs.

Melons Melba   (Serves 6 to 8)

1 package frozen raspberries
½ cup currant jelly
2 teaspoons cornstarch

2 tablespoons water
½ teaspoon almond extract
6 cups melon balls or chunks

Heat raspberries and currant jelly to boiling. Blend cornstarch with water. Stir into raspberry mixture. Simmer until mixture thickens. Add almond extract. Strain and cool. Spoon chilled melon balls into sherbet glasses. Top with sauce.

IX

The Elegant Eight

According to Brillat-Savarin (and *who* could offer a cookbook without at least one quote from him), "Alcohol is the king of potables, and carries to the nth degree the excitation of our palates." So, contrary to all rules governing the most ancient and snobbish of food societies, start your dinner parties with a good snort of potable excitation. (Or, if you're truly a dedicated gourmet, a glass of champagne or sherry.)

Here are my most captivating dinner menus for eight gourmets.

P.S. Ask the ladies to dress and the men to wear black ties.

Menu I

ENDIVE, CAVIAR, SOUR CREAM
TOURNEDOS, HENRI IV
WILD RICE
SPINACH SOUFFLÉ
DINNER ROLLS
BUTTER LETTUCE WITH CHEESE
PEARS BAKED IN WINE
COFFEE BRÛLOT

TO SERVE:

Vosne-Romanée, Les Malconsorts (French)
  or
Heitz Cellars, Ruby Cabernet (California)
  or
Inglenook, Cabernet Sauvignon (California)

PREPARATION: This is a sit-down buffet. The dining-room table is set for eight and the food is placed on the buffet for the guests to help themselves. Clear the dinner plates and serve the salad as a separate course. Keep salad plates and forks in freezer until ready to use.

Endive, Sour Cream, Caviar (For hors d'oeuvre.)

The endive is Belgium endive and it must be fresh and firm. Carefully separate the leaves, wash and dry. Arrange on a silver dish. Put ½ teaspoon of sour cream on end of each leaf. Gently dab about ⅓ teaspoon good caviar on top of sour cream. Pass during cocktail hour.

Tournedos, Henri IV

½ cup butter
4 egg yolks
Juice of 1 lemon
1 teaspoon vinegar
1 tablespoon tarragon
Pinch paprika
Pinch cayenne pepper
1 teaspoon minced parsley

1 clove garlic, crushed
8 large fresh mushroom caps
1 tablespoon butter
8 artichoke bottoms, fresh if possible
8 fillets of beef
8 slices toast, crusts cut off

Melt ½ cup butter in top of double boiler over hot water. Beat in yolks then lemon juice, vinegar, spices, parsley and garlic. Stir constantly until sauce is thick, about like sour cream. Remove from stove and leave over the hot water while you do the fillets.

Sauté mushroom caps in 1 tablespoon butter. Heat artichokes in their liquid if canned or water if fresh. In large iron skillet, heat very hot, fry fillets about 3 minutes on each side.

To serve, put toast on hot platter, then a fillet on each piece of toast. Top meat with artichoke bottom, spoonful of sauce, and mushroom cap.

Wild Rice

Prepare according to directions on box before the guests arrive and keep warm over hot water.

Spinach Soufflé

This is *easy* and one of the best recipes in the book.

1½ tablespoons butter
1½ tablespoons flour
½ cup milk
2 cups, cooked, chopped spinach
   (either 2 boxes frozen or 3 or
   4 fresh bunches)

½ cup mayonnaise
3 eggs well beaten
1 clove garlic, crushed
Seasoned salt to taste
1 tablespoon Parmesan cheese

Make white sauce with butter, flour and milk. Add the rest of the ingredients and pour into a greased casserole. Bake at 350° F. for 45 minutes. (Prepare ahead of time and put in oven after guests have arrived. Time it to come out just at serving time.

Butter Lettuce with Cheese

It is sometimes called limestone lettuce. Check your market.

Wash the leaves and leave them whole. Drain and put in plastic bag in refrigerator.

Mix greens quickly with dressing and serve on glass plates with a triangle of mild cheese, Gruyère or Muenster, on the side.

Dressing

2 tablespoons lemon juice
2 tablespoons vinegar
¾ cup olive oil
1 teaspoon seasoned salt

¼ teaspoon pepper
½ teaspoon paprika
½ teaspoon A-1 Sauce
1 clove garlic, crushed

½ teaspoon sugar

Mix in blender and store in glass jar.

Pears Baked in Wine

8 unpeeled pears
8 whole cloves

2 cups Gallo Hearty Burgundy
1 cup water

1 cup sugar

Stick a clove in stem end of each pear. Put pears into a deep casserole and cover with the liquids mixed with the sugar. Bake covered in hot oven (400° F.) for 30 minutes. Uncover and bake for 20 minutes longer. Baste frequently with the sauce. Good either hot or cold.

Coffee Brûlot

2 thin slices lemon with rind
2 thin slices orange with rind
10 whole cloves

3 sticks cinnamon, broken in
   pieces
3 cubes sugar

Into chafing dish put lemon slices, orange slices, cloves and cinnamon.

Bring to table with pot of strong coffee (silver pot of course), bottle of brandy, a metal ladle and 3 cubes of sugar. Pour about ½ cup brandy over contents in chafing dish. Put sugar cubes in ladle, fill to top with brandy and hold over lighted candle on table to heat. Don't be in a hurry. When brandy is good and warm, lower ladle so flame from candle will ignite brandy. Let burn for a minute then pour into chafing dish. Pour in very hot coffee, mix with ladle, serve in demitasse cups.

Menu II

QUICHE LORRAINE (page 76)
LOBSTER THERMIDOR
GUMBO GOUTER
HEARTS-OF-PALM SALAD
MONKEY BREAD
CHEESECAKE EDNA CORA
COFFEE ANISETTE

TO SERVE:

This dinner has such delicate flavors that you should not begin with cocktails. Instead, serve wine with the quiche:

Charles Krug, Sylvaner (California)

WITH DINNER:

Le Clos, Chablis (French)

or

Charles Krug, Traminer (California)

or

Gallo, Chablis Blanc (California)

PREPARATION: Dinner is served on two tables for four in the living room. Most department stores now carry table "rounds" that convert card tables into round dinner tables. Make or buy cloths that hang to the floor.

Cut the quiche into wedges as you would a pie, and serve warm on tiny dessert plates with a salad or dessert fork. Serve it in the living room with the chilled Sylvaner as you would at a regular cocktail hour.

As salad and dinner plates are served at the same time, this is quite a simple dinner to handle. And while he pours the chilled white wine at dinner, you pass the hot monkey bread.

Lobster Thermidor

½ stick butter
3 tablespoons flour
½ cup cream
¼ teaspoon salt
¼ teaspoon red pepper
½ teaspoon paprika
½ teaspoon dry mustard
Dash of Worcestershire
2 egg yolks

2 tablespoons sherry
½ teaspoon vinegar
1 tablespoon lemon juice
Lobster meat
8 lobster shells (half lobster)
½ pound fresh mushrooms, sliced thin
½ cup bread crumbs
¼ cup grated cheese

2 tablespoons chopped chives

Melt butter and add flour. Stir. Add cream very slowly and cook until thick. Add salt, pepper, paprika, mustard and Worcestershire. Take off fire and add yolks, sherry, vinegar and lemon juice. Add lobster meat and mushrooms. Spoon into empty shells, sprinkle with crumbs, cheese and chives and place under broiler for 10 minutes.

Gumbo Goûter

2 tablespoons salad oil
1 large eggplant, peeled and cut in chunks
3 bell peppers
½ pound okra
2 large onions

1 clove garlic
1 small can tomatoes
½ teaspoon sugar
¼ teaspoon salt
¼ teaspoon cayenne
¼ teaspoon pepper

Cut up vegetables. Heat oil in pan. When hot, put in vegetables. Add rest of ingredients, cover tightly and simmer for 1½ hours. Stir often and check for dryness. Add a little water if needed.

Add shrimp to this sometime and you have a first-rate gumbo.

Hearts-of-Palm Salad

1 head butter lettuce
2 cans palm hearts (Store overnight in the refrigerator.)
4 hard-boiled eggs
½ cup olive oil
2 tablespoons wine vinegar

1 tablespoon lemon juice, fresh
1 teaspoon curry powder
¼ teaspoon salt and pepper
2 tablespoons capers
1 tablespoon Worcestershire

Wash and dry lettuce leaves. Divide among 6 individual salad plates.

On leaves arrange palm hearts and egg slices. Mix remaining ingredients and pour over all.

Monkey Bread

1½ packages of yeast	1 teaspoon salt
1 cup milk	½ cup butter, melted
4 tablespoons sugar	3½ cups flour

Dissolve the yeast in the milk which should be scalded and cooled to lukewarm. Stir in the rest of the ingredients and beat well. Cover with a towel and let rise in a warm place until double in bulk. Punch down and roll out on a floured board to ¼-inch thickness. Cut into 2½-inch diamonds and dip in butter. Arrange overlapping in a medium ring mold (mold will be half full) and let rise again. Bake in 400° F. oven for 30 minutes or until golden brown.

Cheesecake Edna Cora

6 double graham crackers (the cinnamon kind if possible)	½ teaspoon vanilla
½ stick butter, melted	1 small can crushed pineapple, drained
2 eggs	Carton sour cream
½ cup sugar	2 tablespoons sugar
¾ pound Philadelphia cream cheese (8-oz. and 4-oz. pkg.)	Dash of cinnamon

Between two pieces of wax paper roll the graham crackers fine (with a rolling pin). Mix with the melted butter and 2 tablespoons sugar. Pat with a fork into a Pyrex pie pan to form a crust.

Mix with beater 2 eggs, ½ cup sugar, Philadelphia cream cheese and vanilla. Drain pineapple and add with a couple of extra strokes. Pour into the pie shell and bake for 20 minutes at 375° F. Cool for 1 hour. Mix sour cream with 2 tablespoons sugar and a dash of cinnamon and frost the top of the pie. Bake for 5 minutes at 375° F. to set. Cool again.

NOTE: Edna Cora is my mother and quite a cook in her own right.

Coffee Anisette

Put a tablespoon of brandy and a teaspoon of anisette into each cup of coffee and float a lemon twist on top.

Menu III

ARTICHOKES WITH BABY SHRIMP
STEAK TERIYAKI
MADRAS FRUIT CURRY WITH RICE
ONION AND CHEESE MUFFINS
CHERRY PORT SALAD
CRÊME BRULÉE
COFFEE

TO SERVE:

Jadot, Beaujolais (French)

or

Buena Vista, Zinfandel (California)

or

Mondavi, Cabernet Sauvignon (California)

PREPARATION: Serve this dinner buffet either in the living room or dining room. (I once attended a black-tie dinner that was held in a bedroom. It was Academy Awards night and that's where the color TV was. The guests sat on a big fur-covered bed, the floor and a velvet chaise longue. After the presentations we played charades, then turned out the lights and told horror stories. Actually our show was far better than the one we were asked to view!)

Artichokes with Baby Shrimp (This is the hors d'oeuvre)

3 medium artichokes, cooked and cooled

1 pound tiny shrimp (sometimes called bay or brine shrimp)

Mayonnaise flavored with curry

Separate the artichoke leaves, dip the end of each one in mayonnaise and put on silver platter. Place several baby shrimp on each leaf.

Steak Teriyaki

2½ pounds of sirloin, tenderloin or fillet

2 teaspoons ground ginger.

2 tablespoons sugar

1 cup soy sauce

¼ cup molasses

1 cup burgundy

2 large cloves garlic, crushed

Place meat in flat Pryrex pan. Make a marinade of everything else and pour over. Let stand as long as possible. Broil.

Madras Fruit Curry with Rice

Prepare plain boiled white rice for 8 according to directions on package. Keep warm until needed. To serve heap on large platter and cover with a selection of fresh fruit: pineapple pieces, melon balls, grapes, strawberries, peaches, bananas. Over this, ladle the following sauce:

2 cups dry white wine
1½ cups chicken broth (Use bouillon cubes, if necessary.)
2 tablespoons curry powder

1½ tablespoons cornstarch
⅓ cup raisins
¼ cup slivered almonds

Combine wine and broth and heat until simmering. Mix curry and cornstarch with enough water to moisten and add. Simmer for 5 minutes more.

Pour over the fruit and sprinkle with raisins and slivered almonds.

If you can't find fresh fruit, try this canned variation. It can even be made the day before and refrigerated.

⅓ cup butter
¾ cup brown sugar
4 teaspoons curry powder
1 large can pears halves, at least 10 ounces

5 maraschino cherries
1 medium can pineapple chunks, about 6 ounces
1 large can apricot halves, at least 10 ounces

Heat oven to 325° F. In pan, melt butter, add sugar and curry, and stir. Drain fruit and dry on a paper towel. Arrange fruit on heat-proof dish and pour sugar mixture over. Bake for 1 hour. If made the day before, bake and refrigerate. Reheat in oven for 20 minutes before serving over warm rice.

Onion and Cheese Muffins

3 cups biscuit mix
1 teaspoon onion salt
1 cup shredded Cheddar cheese

1¼ cups milk
1 3½-ounce can of French fried onion rings, crumbled

Combine biscuit mix, salt, cheese and milk. Stir until all is moistened. Stir in the onions and spoon into greased muffin tins. Bake at 400° F. for 15 minutes or until golden brown. Enough for 12 muffins.

Cherry Port Salad

1 can sweet dark cherries, pitted   ¾ cup port wine
1 package black cherry Jello   ½ cup chopped nut meats

Strain the juice from the cherries and heat it in pan until it boils. Remove from heat and stir in Jello until it dissolves. Add wine and let stand in refrigerator until it begins to set. Stir in cherries and nuts and put into ring mold. Chill until firm.

Dressing for Salad

1 small package cream cheese   Enough orange juice to make
1 teaspoon sugar   cheese pourable.

Crème Brulée

2 cups (1 pint) whipping cream   2 tablespoons brandy
6 egg yolks   1 teaspoon vanilla
¼ cup sugar   ½ cup toasted chopped almonds
⅛ teaspoon salt   ¾ cup light brown sugar

Heat cream over low flame until scalded. Beat yolks with the sugar and salt. Gradually stir the hot cream into the egg mixture. Put into top of double boiler and place over hot water. Cook and stir constantly until mixture coats the back of spoon. Remove from heat and place pan in cold water to cool quickly. Stir in brandy, vanilla and toasted almonds. Pour into heat-proof baking dish and chill, uncovered, until dinner time. Just before serving, press sugar through sieve with the back of wooden spoon and cover top of pudding with it. Make sure none of the pudding shows through. Sugar coating should be about ¼ inch thick.

Set the baking dish in an oven-proof pan of crushed ice and place under a preheated broiler just until sugar caramelizes. Watch it! This takes just a couple of seconds.

To serve, break through the crust with a spoon, keeping as much of it on top of custard as possible. Serve plain or with a cookie on the side. For a different taste spoon fresh berries over the top.

Menu IV

COQUILLES SAINT-JACQUES
CRAB-AND-SHRIMP BEIRUT
ARTICHOKES ROCKEFELLER
RICE ALMONDINE
ENGLISH MUFFINS
CHEZ VOLTAIRE SALAD
COFFEE MOUSSE WITH STRAWBERRIES
COFFEE

TO SERVE: With Coquilles Saint-Jacques:
Almadén Champagne, Blanc de Blancs (California)

WITH DINNER:

Jadot, Corton-Charlemagne (French) or
Charles Krug, Traminer (California) or
Concannon, Sauvignon Blanc (California)

PREPARATION: Discourage cocktails. Begin in the living room with the
Coquilles and champagne. This is a sit-down dinner so fill the plates
in the kitchen unless you have someone to serve. The salad can be
prepared ahead and either put on the table with the entrée or served
separately.

Coquilles Saint-Jacques

1½ cups water	4 tablespoons flour
½ cup white wine	1 clove garlic, crushed
1 teaspoon salt	1 tablespoon chopped parsley
¼ teaspoon cayenne	2 egg yolks, beaten
2 pints scallops	1½ cups fresh bread crumbs,
½ stick butter	buttered
1 onion chopped fine	½ cup grated Parmesan cheese

In skillet combine water, wine, salt and cayenne. Simmer the scallops
in this for 5 minutes, then fish them out and chop fine. Reserve the
broth.

Melt butter in the empty skillet and sauté the onion until tender.
Add flour stirring into broth a little at a time until sauce thickens. Add

garlic and parsley and cook, stirring constantly, for 5 minutes. Gently stir sauce into beaten egg yolks a bit at a time. Add scallops and heat gently.

Pour into individual scallop shells, top with crumbs mixed with cheese and bake in 425° F. oven until brown (about 5 minutes).

Crab and Shrimp Beirut

½ stick butter
3 tablespoons flour
½ pint cream
1 can consommé
½ tablespoon horseradish
1 teaspoon dry mustard
1 tablespoon catsup
4 tablespoons sherry

1 clove garlic, crushed
Juice of ½ lime
1 teaspoon salt
2 teaspoons Accent
1 pound crab meat, cooked
1 pound shrimp, cleaned and cooked
¼ cup chopped parsley

Melt butter in large Dutch oven. Slowly add flour while stirring with wire whisk. Heat cream and consommé together and add to butter, stirring until smooth. Add everything else but the parsley. If sauce is too thin, thicken with a little cornstarch mixed with water. To thin, add milk. Serve over rice and sprinkle with chopped parsley.

Artichokes Rockefeller

8 artichoke bottoms
8 whole mushrooms with stems removed

Creamed spinach (see below)
Topping (see below)

Part I:

2 packages frozen chopped spinach

½ pound chopped mushrooms
3 tablespoons butter

Cook and drain spinach. Melt butter in saucepan and sauté mushrooms. Add to spinach.

Part II:

2 tablespoons butter
1 tablespoon flour

½ cup milk
1 clove garlic

Make a cream sauce with butter, flour and milk. Then add 1 clove garlic, crushed.

Add spinach to cream sauce.

Part III:

1 small carton sour cream   1 cup mayonnaise
                    Juice of large lemon

Mix all together in saucepan and heat slowly. This is the topping.
Assemble:
Arrange 8 canned artichoke bottoms in large Pyrex pan. On each put
a scoop of creamed spinach, a spoonful of topping and whole mushroom
cap that has been sautéed in butter. Bake for 15 minutes at 375° F.

Rice Amandine

½ cup butter   3 cubes beef bouillon dissolved
1½ cups rice   in 3 cups hot water
2 teaspoons seasoned salt   1 small package chopped
1 small clove garlic, crushed   almonds, about ½ cup
¼ teaspoon seasoned pepper

Melt butter in iron skillet. Add rice. Cook slowly, stirring until rice
turns brown. Transfer into casserole or pot with a lid and add everything else. Mix and bake, covered, for 1 hour in 300° F. oven. Do not
stir while baking.

Chez Voltaire Salad

4 bunches watercress, chopped   2 green peppers, diced
   fine   4 small green onions, chopped,
4 tomatoes, diced   tops and all

Mix all together in bowl with vinegar-and-oil dressing. Serve in
individual bowls set on a salad plate.

Coffee Mousse with Strawberries

1 envelope unflavored gelatin   1 teaspoon freshly grated orange
½ cup cold water   peel or ½ teaspoon Spice Is-
1 tablespoon instant coffee   land dried orange peel
6 eggs   1½ cups heavy cream, whipped
1 13-ounce can evaporated milk,   (½ pint)
   sweetened with 4 tablespoons   2 or 3 cups strawberries, whole
   sugar   4 tablespoons Cointreau

Soften gelatin in cold water, then dissolve over hot water. Stir in
coffee. Set aside to cool.

Beat eggs well until thick and lemon-colored. Add milk and orange peel and beat until well blended.

Stir in gelatin mixture. Whip 1 cup cream and fold in gently. Pour into a ring mold and chill until set (overnight or about 8 hours).

Wash and hull strawberries. Place in small bowl, pour 3 tablespoons Cointreau over them, and set aside.

When ready to serve, dip, mold quickly in hot water and invert on serving dish. Blend 1 tablespoon Cointreau with ½ cup whipped cream.

Pile the cream and half the berries into center of mousse. Use rest of berries to go around mousse for decoration. To serve, cut mold into serving pieces and spoon on berries and whipped cream.

Menu V

SHRIMP RÉMOULADE

EYE OF BEEF FILLET, BARBECUED

HOT MUSHROOM PIE

ONIONS ITALIANO

SALAD WINDSOR

OLIVE FOLD-OVERS

BELGIAN LE BLANCH

COFFEE

TO SERVE:

Chateau Latour (French)

or

Cariñena Clarete (Spanish)

or

Charles Krug, Cabernet Sauvignon (California)

PREPARATION: Plan to give this dinner party during the balmy summer months. Set the table on the terrace with the best silver and crystal. Use only candlelight. Serve the shrimp with cocktails while the fillet cooks on the grill.

Shrimp Rémoulade

2½ pounds cooked shrimp
1 cup salad oil
½ cup horseradish mustard
⅓ cup white wine
2 teaspoons seasoned salt
2 teaspoons paprika

2 teaspoons Tabasco sauce
2 hard-boiled eggs, chopped
1 cup chopped celery
¼ cup chopped parsley
3 green onions, chopped
½ green pepper, chopped

Shell and devein the cooked shrimp. Combine salad oil with mustard, wine, salt, paprika and Tabasco sauce. Beat until well blended and add chopped eggs, celery, parsley, green onion and pepper. Add shrimp and mix well. Cover and place in refrigerator for 12 hours, stirring once in a while. Drain off marinade and serve shrimp in individual scallop shells with tiny cocktail forks.

Eye of Beef Fillet, Barbecued

Ask your butcher for a whole eye of fillet. Prepare your barbecue as you would for steaks. This is a lean cut of meat, so keep turning and brushing with a mixture of half olive oil and half melted butter. If you like, have the butcher lard the meat, but this costs more, naturally. It will take about 30 minutes to grill the fillet for serving rare. (Just assume that all your guests prefer their meat rare. If there are some who don't, return their slices to the grill and cook a few minutes longer.)

Place the fillet on a handsome wooden patter, surround with watercress and, place on table. Carve nice thick slices. Put a pat of garlic butter in the center of each slice and let it melt on its way to the diner.

Mushroom Pie

1 pound fresh mushrooms
¼ cup butter
3 tablespoons minced shallots
¼ cup flour
1 cup cream

1 can beef broth
Salt
Pepper
2 tablespoons sherry
Pastry dough

Clean mushrooms, slice, leaving stems on, and sauté gently in butter for 5 minutes along with the minced shallots. Add flour, cook 2 minutes longer, then pour in cream and beef broth. Season with salt, pepper and sherry. Cook until thick and smooth (but not too thick.) Pour into deep-dish plate or casserole; cover with pastry, like a pie. Brush top of pie with cream, slash so steam will escape and bake in 450° F. oven for 15 minutes.

For pastry I use ½ recipe packaged piecrust mix, substituting cream for water. The pie is better with honest-to-goodness real pastry top, of course, but I need that extra time to put on my false eyelashes.

This recipe also makes an excellent hors d'oeuvre to serve from the coffee table in the living room.

NOTE: One single shallot makes about 1 teaspoon minced. Look for smallish single shallots, not fat ones in "clusters" like garlic. I find the soft green stems in center of fat ones don't mince well.

Onions Italiano

1 pound tiny pearl onions	½ teaspoon thyme
1½ cups water	1 teaspoon chopped parsley
½ cup white wine vinegar	½ cup seedless raisins
3 tablespoons olive oil	2 tablespoons sugar
3 tablespoons tomato paste	Salt
1 bay leaf	Pepper

Peel onions and put into pan with rest of ingredients. Cook slowly for 30 minutes. Chill. Serve in large cutglass bowl to accompany meat.

Salad Windsor

1 large head romaine, torn in pieces	½ cup pitted ripe olives, chopped (they come in cans already chopped.)
1 large head curly endive, torn in pieces	1 can rolled anchovies, boneless
2 glass jars artichoke hearts, drained (about 3 ounces)	2 tomatoes, cut in wedges

Mix all together in large salad bowl. Toss with ⅓ of the dressing until all ingredients are coated. Pass rest of dressing.

Dressing

1 cup mayonnaise	3 tablespoons anchovy paste
½ cup sour cream	3 tablespoons vinegar
⅓ cup snipped parsley	1 tablespoon lemon juice

Dash freshly ground pepper

Put all together in blender and mix.

Olive Fold-overs

1 can refrigerator biscuits (or 2   1 egg yolk
   cans if you think guests will eat   ¼ cup milk
   more than one apiece)   Stuffed green olives

Open cans and flatten each biscuit with your hands. Butter generously and fold over. Brush tops with yolk beaten with milk and firmly press a slice of stuffed olive onto each one. Bake in 450° F. oven for 15 to 20 minutes or until golden brown.

Belgian Le Blanch

1 package vanilla pudding   1¾ cups milk
1½ cups milk   ½ pint whipping cream
   ¾ cup crème de menthe   Piece of semisweet chocolate for
1 package chocolate pudding   grating

Prepare the vanilla pudding according to directions, but use only 1½ cups milk. When thick, remove from fire and stir in ¼ cup of crème de menthe. Fill 8 dessert glasses ½ full and set aside to cool.

Make chocolate pudding using 1¾ cups milk. When thick, remove from fire and add ¼ cup crème de menthe and stir well and set aside to cool. Fill the dessert glasses ½ full of the vanilla pudding. Top with the chocolate pudding.

Whip the cream, flavor with final ¼ cup crème de menthe and put dollop on top of each glass. Grate semisweet chocolate over the top of the cream.

X

Theme Dinners and Costume Parties

The secret of entertaining people in large numbers is organization. And when you entertain for your man you'd better be organized! Here is a checklist that has saved my neck more than once:

One Month Before

1. Don't give a party for over 20 people without a warm body to help in the kitchen. Clear the date with her before you even send out invitations.

2. Put a "please reply" on the bottom of the invitation. Too few people can be as devastating as too many.

3. Arrange for live music, if you can afford it. If not, be sure you have put together a lively collection of records.

The Week Before

1. Plan your menu. Don't include anything you haven't tried before; or at least have a working idea of how to go about making it.

2. Work out the mechanics of chairs, serving tables, dance space, etc., and borrow or rent what you need.

3. Count dishes, silver, napkins, glasses, etc., and borrow or rent what you don't have.

4. Decide what you are going to wear and see if it needs cleaning.

Two Days Before

1. Set up tables and do the decorating. Most fresh cut flowers will last a couple of days.

2. Make a complete check of all items listed in the recipes on your menu. Don't forget spices and herbs, bases, etc.

3. Make a giant list of everything you need.

4. Ask your husband to check the bar and give you a list of mixes, olives, onions, etc., that he needs. Add these to your list. Remind him to order wine, ice and glasses when he orders the liquor.

The Day Before

1. As soon as the store opens, do your marketing.

2. Prepare the cook-ahead items while you sort and store food.

3. Put out cigarettes, ashtrays and cocktail napkins.

4. Put out plates, serving dishes and flat silver.

5. Go to the hairdresser's.

6. Ask your darling husband to take you out to dinner.

The Day Of

1. Finish cooking whatever needs to be cooked.

2. Clean up the kitchen.

3. Call himself and double check on liquor and ice.

4. Pour yourself a wee drop and sip slowly while you soak in the tub.

5. Put on your velvet culottes.

6. Light the candles.

7. Put out cold hors d'oeuvres.

8. Smile.

The Mexican Fiesta . . . "Buen Provecho" . . .

This is a dinner party that you can serve in the dining room at one long table or in the living room on several card tables. A nice time of the year to do this is at Christmas. Your party then becomes a Posada. And the hot Mexican food is a welcome contrast to the bland or terribly rich fare usually offered at this time of year.

Ask the women guests to wear long skirts or hostess pajamas, the men sport shirts. And of course, play Mexican and Spanish records. If you are using this for one of your major parties of the year, double or triple your guest list and hire two or three guitarists for the evening.

Menu for Mexican Fiesta for Twelve

MARGUERITAS
CHILI CON QUESO
POLLO ADOBADO
COLIFLOR CON GUACAMOLE
PAN DE ELOTA
SPINACH SALAD
CARTA BLANCA CERVEZA
BESO DE KALUHA
CAFÉ DIABLO

Margueritas

For this many people, buy the mix and make accordingly. Ice the glasses and dip rims in salt.

Chili con Queso

The easiest version of this recipe is to melt a large jar of Cheez Whiz. Then add a small can of diced Ortega Chilis. Serve warm with tortilla chips. Put a knife beside the bowl on the table because cheese hardens as it cools.

If there is any left over, put it in the refrigerator and use it for sandwiches, for Mexican cheeseburgers, or melted over vegetables. It gets hotter the longer you keep it.

Pollo Adobado

For 12 people, have your butcher bone and halve twelve chicken breasts. There may be some left over, but they are great, even when eaten cold. Flour the chicken by shaking it in a bag containing flour, salt and pepper.

Sauté chicken in a heavy iron skillet in hot olive oil and butter, equal parts. The chicken should be brown but not hard and crusty. Transfer the pieces to the earthenware or Mexican casserole in which you are going to serve them. Cover with sauce:

Sauce

3 cups freshly squeezed orange juice	6 tablespoons sugar
	3 teaspoons cinnamon
1½ cups raisins	1½ teaspoons ground cloves
1 large can crushed pineapple (8 to 10 ounces)	1 small bottle dry white wine (Chablis is good)

Mix all together and pour over chicken. Cover the casserole and bake for ½ hour at 350° F. If your casserole doesn't have a lid, cover with aluminum foil. Make in the morning and reheat to serve.

Coliflor con Guacamole   (Serves 12)

Cook two medium heads of cauliflower, whole, in boiling salted water for 10 to 15 minutes. You want them to be still a bit crisp. Drain the heads and turn them upside down in two bowls. Pour an oil-and-vinegar dressing over them, about ½ bottle to each head. If you prefer, make your own dressing, but bottled is so easy. Do this in the morning, then frost just before serving.

Guacamole Frosting

2 cans frozen avocado dip	½ small carton sour cream
⅓ cup fresh lemon juice	Salt
½ cup dry chopped onions	Pepper
Dash Tabasco	

Mix all the above together and beat with an electric hand mixer or put in blender. Just before serving, frost the cauliflower with this exactly as you would frost a cake. Serve whole on platters with a knife to cut it.

Pan de Elota   (Serves 12)

2 cans creamed corn	2 teaspoons baking soda
2 cups yellow cornmeal	2 teaspoons salt
2 eggs	1½ cups milk
⅔ cup melted butter	

Mix all the above together and store in refrigerator.

One hour before dinner, pour half the batter into a large greased Mexican casserole (or two Pyrex casseroles). Cover the batter with:

1 small can Ortega diced chilies
1 cup grated mild yellow cheese

Pour in the other half of the batter and cover with another can of chilies and another cup of cheese. Bake at 350° F. for 45 minutes. (If you are making it in the two glass dishes, don't cook it quite so long.)

This has the consistency of spoon bread and is dished up with a large wooden spoon. It gets firmer as it cools. The leftovers can be removed from the casserole the next day and reheated with a little water in a covered saucepan. You can also reheat the chicken and sauce and serve it over the corn bread the next day.

Beso de Kaluha

In small dessert bowls or even wooden salad bowls, put a scoop of vanilla ice cream. Top with a jigger of Kaluha and a teaspoonful of sliced almonds. Fix in the kitchen and serve from a large tray.

Café Diablo

In the morning, put three thin slices of unpeeled orange and unpeeled lemon into a chafing dish. Stick three or four cloves in each slice. Put twelve lumps of sugar and six or eight sticks of cinnamon in with the fruit. Make a pot of coffee. Just before ready to serve, reheat the coffee. Fill a ladle with about ½ cup brandy, heat over a candle, ignite and pour into chafing dish. After it burns a minute, pour in good, strong, hot coffee. Stir and ladle into demitasse cups or small mugs.

ORGY OR LOVE-IN FOR SIXTEEN PEOPLE

This party should be a hot-weather party outside. Guests must wear togas, caftans or come as flower children.

Go to a thrift shop and buy some old card tables. Saw the legs off about six or eight inches from the top. Set up in a row on the grass.

Cover with white cloths or sheets (I use old ones, dyed lavender) and trail ivy and all kinds of greenery down the middle. Add bunches of grapes tied with purple ribbon and whatever flowers happen to be handy. Use bright pillows to sit on.

Menu for Orgy or Love-In for Sixteen

OUZO COOLERS
IMAM BAILDI MEZE
PSARI PLAKE
DOLMADES
SPANAKORIZO
SALTA THERMOPILE
GREEK PASTRIES OR TOURTA ME AMYGTHALA
GREEK COFFEE

Don't be put off by a few Greek names—you can make anything listed here right in your kitchen in Duluth or Atlanta. And they're all delicious.

TO SERVE WITH DINNER:
Domestica (Greek)
  or
Retzina (Greek)
  or
Nebbiolo, Piedmontese (Italian)
  or
Sabastiani, Barbera (California)

AFTER DINNER:
Achaia-Clauss (Greek Brandy)

Ouzo Coolers

Ouzo is an anise-flavored Greek aperitif. Serve over ice cubes. Great. Really sets the pace for the party.

Imam Baildi Meze

You can buy a passable eggplant dip in a can and mix with it a bit of olive oil and some capers. Or make this:

1 eggplant	3 cloves garlic, crushed
1 cup olive oil	1 tablespoon chopped parsley
3 large onions, sliced	3 tablespoons capers
3 large tomatoes, chopped	2 tablespoons sliced stuffed olives

Make in the morning on the day of the party or the day before. Store in refrigerator.

Peel and cut eggplant in strips. Fry in ½ cup olive oil for 2 to 3 minutes.

Add the rest of the oil and everything but capers and olives plus about ½ cup water. Simmer with lid on until eggplant is soft. Add water if mixture gets dry. Watch carefully. Takes about 30 minutes.

Remove from heat and cool. Mash with potato masher. Add capers and olives and serve cold with flat bread from Greek bakery.

Psari Plaki   (Serves 16)

About 3 or 4 pounds of a good baking fish, such as sea bass or halibut. You need enough fish to fill two recetangular Pyrex cake pans.

Salt	6 green onions, chopped with
Pepper	tops
Paprika	2 cups chopped parsley
Oregano	4 onions, cut in rings
1 cup olive oil	40 saltine crackers
4 cloves garlic	Butter
6 tomatoes, sliced	Lemon slices
Water	

In the morning, grease the baking pan and arrange the fish either whole or cut in pieces. Sprinkle with salt and pepper, paprika and oregano. Pour ½ cup olive oil over each pan. Crush garlic over the fish.

Arrange tomato slices over fish and sprinkle with green onions and parsley. Add onion rings and few thin slices of lemon. Place crackers, a few at a time, between pieces of wax paper and with rolling pin, crush fine. Or put in blender. Sprinkle over fish. Wrap in Saran and store in refrigerator.

Two hours before dinner, remove from the refrigerator and let stand at room temperature for an hour or so. When ready to cook, put ½ cup water in each pan and bake in preheated 350° F. oven for 45 minutes.

Dolmades

1½ pound ground lamb
1¼ cup uncooked white rice
1 medium onion, chopped

1 can (8 ounce) tomato paste
1 large lemon
2 jars grape leaves

Mix lamb, rice, onion, and 4 tablespoons tomato paste. Add juice of one large lemon. Carefully unwrap and wash each leaf under running water. Put a teaspoon of meat mixture on each leaf and wrap up in envelope fold.

Line a large earthenware casserole with extra leaves, laid flat, and pour in 3 tablespoons of tomato sauce. Arrange and stack the stuffed leaves in the casserole. Pour over top ¼ cup tomato sauce mixed with ¼ cup water. Store in refrigerator until needed. Cover and bake in 350° F. oven for 35 to 45 minutes.

If you have any left from the party, they make a superb cold hors d'oeuvre.

Spanakorizo   (Serves 16)

5 onions, chopped
3 cloves garlic, minced
2 green peppers, chopped
2 cups olive oil
1 small can tomato paste (4 to 6 ounces)

6 packages frozen chopped spinach
1½ cups rice
3 cups bouillon (cubes dissolved in hot water are fine)
1 teaspoon salt

1 teaspoon pepper

In large Dutch oven, sauté the onions, garlic and peppers in oil. Add tomato paste, cooked and drained spinach and stir. Add bouillon and heat to boiling. Add salt and pepper. Sprinkle rice on top. Do not mix. Cover and gently simmer until rice is done. About 25 to 35 minutes.

Salta Thermopile

All kinds of lettuce, chickory, endive, etc., washed, dried and pulled into pieces. Enough needed to fill two large wooden salad bowls. Fix in the morning and store in refrigerator in towel.

When ready to serve, add sliced cucumbers, parsley, anchovies, large Greek olives and bits of white Greek cheese. (I always have bowls of olives and feta cheese on the table, too.) Just fix as you would a regular tossed salad. Mix with vinegar, lemon juice, olive oil and plenty of salt (3 parts oil to 1 part vinegar and lemon juice).

Greek Pastries

At a good Greek bakery buy 16 delicious pastries or make:

Tourta Me Amygthala

Make the day before. Nothing about this recipe is a snap, but it is the best way I've found to do it. Buy a roll of sugar-cookie dough in the delicatessen section of the market. Thaw dough if frozen. Unwrap, put between pieces of wax paper and roll out to fit oblong 9 × 13-inch pan. Chill dough and start over if it becomes too sticky. Dough must be thin as piecrust.

If you don't want to do it this way, make up your own recipe of sugar-cookie dough and use that.

Filling

8 eggs	8 zwieback, crushed
1 cup sugar	1 teaspoon almond extract
1 cup chopped blanched almonds	½ teaspoon salt

⅓ cup melted butter

Separate eggs. Beat yolks and add sugar. Add nuts, zwieback, extract and salt. Beat whites until firm and fold in. Add butter. Pour on top of cookie dough.

Bake at 350° F. for about 30 to 40 minutes.

You can dribble warmed honey over tourta before serving, which makes it a bit sticky, but good.

TWENTY-TWO-BOY CURRY PARTY FOR FORTY-FOUR

For this party, your female guests are asked to come as seekers of Wisdom and Truth. Each male guest is to come as a guru, and bring an assigned condiment to present. And each must be extremely inventive as he will be judged on originality of thought when presentations are made during cocktail hour.

To serve this dinner, use the cut-off card tables from the Orgy (p. 124) covered with bright cloths and supply pillows to sit on. Have plenty of candles, incense and mystic music. You might hire a fortune teller or palmist for the evening to give psychic readings.

Menu

PIMM'S CUP

SWEET-AND-SOUR MEATBALLS

MALAYAN SHRIMP CURRY

MURGHI CHICKEN CURRY

INDONESIAN BEEF CURRY

RICE

TWENTY-TWO-BOY CONDIMENTS

SALAD NEPAL

PURI

LIQUEUR SUNDAES

FORTUNE COOKIES

COFFEE

TO SERVE:

Ballantine Ale or English Beer

Pimm's Cup

Pimm's cup is always followed by a number: Pimm's cup 1, 2, or 3. The number designates the liquor used as the base of the drink. Go to your favorite liquor store and buy the Pimm's Cup that best serves your palate. Chill. Mix with equal parts cold lemon soda. Float a sliced cucumber on top or make a finger-size swizzle stick from a slice of cucumber.

Sweet-and-sour Meatballs

2 cans water chestnuts (#2-½ can)   ¼ cup soy sauce
5 pounds lean ground pork   6 eggs slightly beaten
3 bunches green onions, chopped   1 tablespoon salt
   (discard tops)   2½ cups bread crumbs

Drain water chestnuts thoroughly and have your butcher put them through the meat grinder once with the pork. Add other ingredients and mix well. Form into tiny balls the size of a large green olive. Fry lightly. This makes over a hundred balls. Make in the morning and leave in bowls on back of stove. Serve with Sweet-and-sour Sauce.

Sweet-and-sour Sauce

1 cup vinegar	2 tablespoons soy sauce
2 cups pineapple juice	3 tablespoons grated ginger
¾ cup sugar	½ cup cornstarch
2 cups canned beef consommé	1 cup cold water

In the morning heat together all ingredients except water and cornstarch; gently heat about 3 to 5 minutes. Mix cornstarch and water and gradually stir into the hot sauce. Keep on back of stove until party. Reheat and add the meat balls. Serve in chafing dishes with toothpicks.

No one curry will serve all, so make three and let guests choose the one or ones they want.

Malayan Shrimp Curry   (Serves 12)

⅔ cup butter	3 chicken bouillon cubes dissolved
1 cup chopped onion	in ½ cup hot water
2 cloves garlic, crushed	4 cups yogurt
2 teaspoons salt	6 pounds cleaned and cooked
2 tablespoons curry powder	shrimp
2 tablespoons flour	

The day before the party, heat butter in skillet and sauté the onion and garlic until soft and lightly browned. Combine salt, curry powder and flour and stir into fat in pan. Gradually add chicken bouillon and stir. Cook for 3 to 4 minutes, stirring constantly. Store until needed.

Reheat just before dinner and stir in yogurt and shrimp. Cook over low heat until warmed through. Put into large casserole for buffet table.

Murghi Chicken Curry   (Serves 16 to 20)

6 fryers, cut up	2 onions, chopped
Giblets	4 cloves garlic, mashed
8 cups water	4 tablespoons curry powder
2 onions, sliced	2 tablespoons salt
2 teaspoons salt	1 teaspoon ground ginger
10 peppercorns	1 teaspoon cinnamon
½ cup flour	½ teaspoon onion salt
1 cup vegetable oil	½ teaspoon pepper
1 stick butter	4 tablespoons lime juice

In the morning, put necks, backs and wings of chickens into large saucepan; add giblets, water, sliced onion, salt and peppercorns. Bring to boil, lower heat and simmer for 40 minutes. Drain and save broth.

Coat remaining pieces of chicken in flour. In large Dutch oven, heat oil and sauté chicken until brown. Remove chicken, empty oil out of pan and heat the butter in the same pan. Sauté the chopped onion and garlic until light brown.

Combine curry powder, 2 teaspoons salt, ginger, cinnamon, onion salt and pepper and stir into butter. Cook 2 or 3 minutes, stirring constantly. Add chicken broth and brown chicken pieces. Cover and simmer for 30 minutes.

Remove chicken, wrap in foil and keep in warm oven. Simmer sauce, uncovered, for 10 to 15 minutes. Add lime juice. Sauce should now be fairly thick.

When ready to serve, arrange chicken on large platter and pour hot sauce over.

Indonesian Beef Curry　　(Serves 8 to 10)

8 tablespoons vegetable oil
4 pounds top round cut in bite-size cubes
3 onions, chopped
5 cloves garlic, crushed
2 teaspoons salt

½ teaspoon pepper
4 tablespoons curry powder
4 cubes bouillon dissolved in 1 cup hot water
3 cups hot water
2 8-ounce cans tomato sauce

2 tablespoons lemon juice

In the morning heat 6 tablespoons of the oil in Dutch oven. Add beef cubes; brown on all sides and remove. Add 2 more tablespoons oil, chopped onion and garlic. Cook until soft and light brown.

Mix together salt, pepper, curry and bouillon. Add to pot and stir for 2 or 3 minutes until well mixed. Add the 3 cups of water, tomato sauce and the browned beef cubes.

Cover and cook over medium heat for 1½ hours. Remove cover and cook for 30 minutes longer or until meat is tender and sauce is thick. Stir in lemon juice. Cover and keep on counter until ready to serve. Reheat if necessary.

Obviously you can't make all three curries at once. Start in the morning and do them one at a time. Everything can be reheated.

Rice

Read the back of a box of rice and you can figure out how much you'll need for forty people. Prepare the rice at the last minute and place a bowl of it next to each curry.

Puri   (Makes 4 dozen)

4½ cups sifted all-purpose flour   2 cups water
2 teaspoons salt   Vegetable oil

Sift flour and salt together into large bowl. Add water to make a stiff dough. Turn out on a well-floured board and knead for about 5 minutes. Dough should be smooth and satiny. Pinch off small pieces of dough (48 in all) and let rest on board for about 20 minutes. Roll each piece of dough paper thin to about 5 inches in diameter.

Pour oil into large skillet 1 inch deep and heat to 390° F. Fry circles of dough, one or two at a time, until golden brown on one side; turn and brown the other. Dough blisters and bubbles in fat.

Drain well on paper towels and serve warm. Make the day of party, not the day before, and reheat in oven if necessary.

Condiments for Twenty-Two-Boy Curry:

1. Chutney
2. Chopped peanuts
3. Flaked coconut
4. Chopped crystalized ginger
5. Crumbled fried-onion rings (canned)
6. Crumbled fried bacon
7. Raisins which have been plumped in hot water
8. Grated orange peel
9. Green onions, tops and all to be chopped
10. Hard-boiled egg, to be chopped.
11. Red apple, unpeeled, to be chopped
12. Cucumber, to be chopped
13. Julienne bananas
14. Green peppers, to be chopped
15. Sunflower seeds

16. Kumquat preserves
17. Tomato relish
18. Candied fruit
19. Green chilies (may be canned), to be chopped
20. Crushed pineapple
21. Pine nuts
22. Olives, to be chopped

How each man prepares his condiment is part of the contest. And he can present condiment in anything from the navel of a brass Buddah to the cup of a live monkey. During the cocktail hour presentation seat guests on the pillows on the floor. Voting is done by applause.

Salad Nepal

Fill three large glass bowls with fresh and canned fruit prepared in advance and stored in covered jars. To serve, mix fruits, pour ginger ale over and sprinkle liberally with chopped preserved ginger. Be sure to include:

Pineapple, mandarine oranges, white grapes, tangerines, apples, and pears, plus any of your choice.

Liqueur Sundaes

Give each guest a dish of vanilla ice cream and pass a tray of liqueurs from which to choose a topping.

LEFT BANK ART SHOW
FOR TWENTY-FOUR

Everyone has at least one friend, husband or lover who paints. (Perhaps one of each?) And probably the nicest thing you could do for a painter or sculptor is to give him a party, showing his work.

Pick a warm dry season, so you can set up the exhibit in the garden. Trees, fences, patio walls all make interesting backdrops. Send invitations made of bright construction paper lettered with felt pen. The theme is French and the dress suggested something guests would wear to a Left Bank showing in Paris.

Menu for Left Bank Showing for Twenty-Four

COCKTAILS OR VERMOUTH AND SODA

OEUFS GLACÉ

JAMBON LA CRÈME

BOEUF BOURGUIGNON

BUTTERED NOODLES OR STEAMED RICE

ANTIPASTO SALAD

FRENCH ROLLS

FRENCH PASTRIES

COFFEE

COGNAC

WINES TO SERVE:

Clos de Vougeot (French)

or

Louis Martini, Pinot Noir (California)

or

Gallo, Hearty Burgundy (California)

Oeufs Glacé

2 tablespoons of gelatin
½ cup water
10 hard-boiled eggs
⅔ cup chow chow (Crosse and Blackwell preferred)

⅔ cup chopped parsley
2 tablespoons Worcestershire sauce
1 teaspoon salt
1 cup mayonnaise

The day before the showing, soften the gelatin in bowl of water, then dissolve it by putting the bowl in a pan of hot water over a low flame. Put hard-boiled eggs through a ricer or rub them through a colander. Mix with other ingredients. You may want to put the chow chow in the blender for a minute so the mold will be "smoother." Stir in gelatin, mix well, and pour into large 2 quart ring mold. Chill.

To serve, unmold on cake stand and fill the center with sour cream. Heap caviar on top of the sour cream and surround the mold with crisp crackers.

Jambon à Crème

4 cans deviled ham (4½ ounce size)

2 tablespoons minced onion
2 tablespoons capers, drained

Mix all together in bowl the day before the showing and keep in refrigerator until ready.

To serve, make a mound of ham on a pedestal cake plate. Frost with mixture of:

1 pound cream cheese	½ cup sour cream
4 teaspoons sharp mustard	

Place platter of tiny rye and pumpernickle rounds next to frost ham mound. Also dish of thin slices of bermuda onions.

Boeuf Bourguignon   (Serves 24)

1 pound bacon, diced	6 onions, chopped
½ cup flour	4 bay leaves
½ teaspoon pepper	2 teaspoons thyme
1 teaspoon salt	4 cups Burgundy
8 pounds chuck, cut into 1-inch cubes	3 pounds fresh mushrooms
8 cloves garlic	½ cup butter
4 leeks, chopped	3 pounds small white onions
6 carrots, chopped	1 cup sherry
	4 teaspoons lemon juice
½ cup chopped parsley	

The day before the showing cook bacon until crisp and brown. Drain. Put flour into a brown paper bag with salt and pepper and drop in the meat cubes, a handful at a time. Shake until coated, then brown in the hot bacon fat. Transfer meat to a large Dutch oven; keep fat in frying pan.

Sauté garlic, carrots and onions in bacon fat until soft and lightly browned. Warm Cognac, ignite and pour over beef. When flame dies, add garlic, leeks, carrots, onions, bay leaf, thyme and Burgundy. Cover and cook for 2 to 2½ hours or until meat is fork-tender.

In another skillet, sauté mushrooms in butter. Remove, then put in and sauté the white onions until brown. Add 1 cup sherry and lemon juice to skillet, cover and simmer onions for 15 minutes. Add mushrooms and onions to meat mixture and cook for 5 minutes more. Keep on back of stove until needed.

To serve, reheat with lots of parsley and put steaming pot on buffet with casserole of buttered noodles or rice next to it.

Antipasto Salad

Romaine   Leaf lettuce
Escarole   Chicory
Dandelion greens, if available

Tear the greens into bite-size pieces as you would for a regular green salad. Dry completely. Rub salad bowl with clove of cut garlic. Make a bed of crisp green in well-chilled salad bowls. For 24, plan on three large bowls.

Antipasto Topping

1 6 to 8-ounce can of tuna,
  drained and broken into chunks
½ can anchovy fillets, cut up
½ cup green olives, sliced
4 hard-boiled eggs, sliced
8 slices salami, diced
1 cup radish slices
2 green peppers, sliced
1 cup minced parsley

1 small jar pimiento strips
8 chopped green onions
2 cans pickled artichoke hearts,
  3 to 4 ounces each
2 jars pickled mushrooms, sliced
  (3 to 6 ounces each)
1 large jar Italian pickled vegetables, drained and sliced
4 tomatoes cut in wedges

Choose any or all of these. Arrange in rows all across the salad. Wrap bowls in Saran and store in refrigerator. Just before serving, add dressing and mix up.

Dressing

½ cup red wine vinegar   1½ cups olive oil

Put in jar with tight lid and shake vigorously.

XI

Food for "Afterwards..."

If your husband's favorite party gesture is to say in a loud voice, "Let's go back to our house and have something to eat," you have to be prepared—at four o'clock in the morning after a charity ball, or three o'clock in the afternoon after a ball game. Preparing your kitchen to handle sudden groups of eaters necessitates an emergency shelf, a freezer, a tidy kitchen (because you *know* that's where everyone will end up), plenty of ice and several clean ruffled aprons.

When He Says—"Come By for Cocktails"

Mexican Turnovers

1 tablespoon cooking oil	½ teaspoon pepper
2 cloves garlic, crushed	2½ tablespoons chili powder
1 medium onion, chopped	1 small can tomato paste
1 pound ground round steak	1 can taco sauce
2 teaspoons salt	1 package piecrust mix

In the morning heat oil in large iron skillet. Simmer the garlic until it starts to darken. Then add everything else but piecrust mix. Cover the pan and simmer slowly for 1 hour. Stir often at the beginning.

When ready to serve, make up the piecrust mix according to directions and roll out ⅛ inch thick. Cut in rounds with a demitasse cup or small biscuit cutter. In middle of each round put a heaping teaspoon of sauce. Fold over and press edges together. Prick with a fork. Place on cookie sheet and bake in 400° F. oven for 15 minutes. The two recipes should come out even—rounds to sauce. But there are never enough, no matter how few you invite.

TO SERVE:

Almadén, Chianti (California)
  or
Gallo, Paisano (California)
  or
Korbel, Pinot Noir (California)

Steak Tartare

1 pound sirloin put through grinder once (1 pound serves 3 to 4 people)
1 tablespoon chopped onion
1 tablespoon chopped parsley

1 tablespoon anchovy paste
1 teaspoon Worcestershire sauce
Dash dry mustard
Freshly ground pepper
1 teaspoon salt

Mix all together and allow flavors to marry. Keep covered in refrigerator until ready to serve. Serve in mound surrounded by toast points.

WINE TO SERVE:

Inglenook, Burgundy (California)

Canapé Antipasto

1 package piecrust mix
6 egg yolks
3 tablespoons soft butter
2 cups sour cream
3 tablespoons flour
1 teaspoon salt

¼ teaspoon garlic salt
1½ cup grated Swiss cheese
1 6-ounce jar stuffed green olives, sliced
1 can sardines
1 tablespoon capers

8 thin slices garlic salami

Mix piecrust according to directions but don't divide. Use all of it. Roll out into an oblong 5 inches by 16 inches or thereabouts. And be sure it is at least ½ inch thick. Place on a cookie sheet and bake for 10 minutes at 425° or until lightly browned. Cool. (Do this ahead of time). Mix together egg yolks, butter, sour cream, flour and salts. Cook over a very low flame, stirring until mixture is smooth and thick. Add cheese and mix smooth. Let cool and store in covered bowl until ready to serve. When guests arrive spread filling evenly over pastry and arrange all the rest of the ingredients on it. Cut in squares and serve.

Mushrooms and Crab

12 large mushrooms, fresh	2 tablespoons horseradish
½ pound crab meat	Juice of ½ lemon
3 tablespoons mayonnaise	2 tablespoons chopped parsley
½ teaspoon salt	½ cup fine bread crumbs
¼ teaspoon pepper	2 tablespoons Parmesan cheese

Mix crab with everything except bread crumbs and cheese. Lightly stuff the mushroom caps and refrigerate until guests arrive.

Sprinkle with bread crumbs mixed with cheese and place under broiler until they brown and bubble.

When He Says "Come By for Dinner" After The Art Show (Serves 6 to 12)

INDIVIDUAL DINNERS COOKED IN HOT CHICKEN BROTH

DISHES OF HOT AND COLD SAUCES

SALAD CICI

HOT CHUNKS OF FRENCH BREAD

CARAMEL SUNDAE

HOT TEA

WINE TO SERVE:

Paul Masson, Rosé (California)

or

Almadén, La Domaine Champagne (California)

or

Inglenook, Semillon (California)

Individual Dinners Cooked in Hot Chicken Broth (Each diner cooks his own.)

2 cans chicken broth	1 cauliflower, cut in bite-size pieces
3 to 6 fillets of beef cut into bite-size pieces	1 package broccoli, cut up
1 to 3 pounds medium shrimp	1 bunch asparagus, cut up
½ to 1 pound fresh mushrooms, small	

Cut up vegetables in the morning and store in refrigerator in plastic sacks. When ready to serve, place an electric fry pan or casserole on a sterno burner in center of table, so all guests can reach it. Don't cut up meat until you count the number of guests.

On stove in kitchen heat chicken broth until boiling and transfer to pot on table. On separate plates for each guest, arrange a selection of meat, shrimp and vegetables. Also supply each guest with a fondue fork or a slotted spoon. Each diner cooks his assortment of raw food in the hot broth and then dips it into one or all of the sauces.

After all the meat, shrimp and vegetables have been cooked by guests, dump a package of very fine noodles into broth and cook for a few minutes. Ladle broth and noodles into mugs and serve. Really makes a delicious "soup" with the flavor from all those things that were cooked in it.

Sauces

Hot Chinese Mustard (canned)   Teriyaki Sauce
            Thousand Island Dressing, etc.

Salad Cici

4 large tomatoes, peeled and finely chopped
2 bunches green onions, finely chopped
4 hard-cooked eggs, finely chopped

12 slices bacon, cooked crisp and crumbled
1 package (3-ounce) blue cheese, crumbled
2 heads iceberg lettuce
2 avocados, finely chopped

Bottle of tart French dressing

The night before the dinner, chop tomatoes. Put in wire strainer and let juice drain. Chop green onions (keeping tops and white part separate) and eggs, crumble the bacon and blue cheese. Store in separate containers in the refrigerator. (If blue cheese is frozen in advance, it will crumble more easily). Just before serving, chop the lettuce and avocado as fine as possible with a sharp vegetable knife. Toss lettuce, eggs, cheese, bacon, white part of onion, avocado and most of the tomato with enough dressing to coat pieces. Arrange on bed of lettuce and garnish with rest of tomato and green onion tops.

Caramel Sundae

Buy a jar of caramel topping, heat and pour over vanilla ice cream. Top with chopped nuts.

When He Says, "Come Back After the Theatre"

Late Supper I   (Serves 6)

MUSHROOMS TERIYAKI
STROGANOFF WITH BUTTERED NOODLES
FINGER ROLLS
FRUIT FRAPPÉ
COFFEE

WINE TO SERVE:

Buena Vista, Cabernet Sauvignon (California)
   or
Gallo, Hearty Burgundy (California)
   or
Christian Brothers, Claret (California)

Mushrooms Teriyaki

12 large mushrooms
½ cup soy sauce
½ pound ground round steak
½ a green pepper, chopped
 2 tablespoons dry fine bread
   crumbs

1 egg yolk
1 clove garlic, crushed
¼ teaspoon each, salt and pepper

This is the hors d'oeuvre.

Remove stems from mushrooms and save. Marinate caps in soy sauce for about 1 hour. If soy sauce doesn't cover, turn occasionally.

Chop mushroom stems fine and mix with all remaining ingredients. Remove mushroom caps from soy sauce, drain and fill with meat mixture. Brush meat with soy sauce. Broil for 8 to 10 minutes.

If you make them in the morning, reheat at 350° F. until heated through. Serve during cocktail time on tiny plates with dessert forks.

NOTE: A good bachelor friend of mine, when he learned I was writing a cookbook, asked me please to tell the single women· to quit serving Stroganoff. It seems to have become the National Dish of the Unmarrieds. My friend said he had it four nights in a row from four separate well-meaning ladies. So I offer this recipe to the firmly engaged or happily married only.

Stroganoff with Buttered Noodles   (Serves 6)

3 tablespoons olive oil
3 tablespoons butter
2½ pounds round steak cut into thin strips
1 large onion, thin sliced
2 cloves garlic, crushed
½ pound fresh mushrooms, thin sliced
1 teaspoon salt
¼ teaspoon pepper
¼ cup red wine
1 small can tomato paste (3 to 4 ounces)
1 bay leaf, crumbled
3 tablespoons flour
2 bouillon cubes dissolved in ½ cup hot water
1 small carton sour cream

Hot buttered noodles

In Dutch oven heat the oil and butter. Brown the strips of beef and remove to another pan. Sauté the onion, garlic and mushrooms until tender. Turn off heat and add salt, pepper, wine, tomato paste, bay leaf and the flour which has been mixed with the bouillon and water until smooth. Stir until ingredients are blended. Add browned meat, cover and bake in 350° F. oven for 1 hour.

When ready to serve, stir in sour cream and reheat. You can make this in the morning. Leave out the sour cream and keep at room temperature. Serve over hot buttered noodles.

Finger Rolls

At the bakery, buy the tiniest rolls you can find—that is a finger roll.

Fruit Frappe   (Serves 6)

2 bananas, diced
Grated peel and juice of 1 lemon
Grated peel and juice of 2 oranges
1 6-ounce can crushed pineapple, drained
¼ cup sugar

2 cups ginger ale

Blend everything together in a bowl. Pour into freezer tray and freeze for 1½ to 2 hours. Stir frequently. Keep in freezer until ready to serve. Serve in chilled champagne glasses.

Late Supper II   (Serves 4)

ROSY CHICKEN

BAKED TOMATOES WITH PEAS

MOLDED CUCUMBER MOUSSE

TINY ROLLS

PORT PARFAIT

COFFEE

WINE TO SERVE:

Schloss, Johannesberg (German) or

Korbel, Brut Champagne (California) or

Beaulieu, Semillon (California)

Rosy Chicken   (Serves 4)

4 chicken breasts, cut and boned   ½ cup butter
(the butcher will do this if you   ½ cup dry white wine
ask him with a smile)   1 tiny jar red-currant jelly
                  1 small carton sour cream

This dinner is cooked and served in front of the fireplace by candle-light after a very romantic play or an especially choice musical. The chicken is cooked in an electric frying pan, so place it near the gathering in front of the fire.

Melt butter in pan and cook chicken at 360° F. for about 15 minutes. Spoon in the jelly and mix with the pan juices. Add sour cream and blend well. Keep turning the chicken until all bubbly and beautifully rosy.

Baked Tomatoes with Peas   (Serves 4)

4 nice large firm tomatoes   ½ teaspoon sugar
1 package frozen peas   ¼ cup fine bread crumbs
1 tablespoon butter   2 tablespoons Parmesan cheese

In the morning, cut tops off tomatoes and scoop out insides. Turn upside down on paper towels to drain. Cook peas according to directions, but add sugar. Drain, mix with butter and put into the tomatoes. Keep in refrigerator until you come home from theatre.

When ready to start cooking dinner, take out tomatoes, sprinkle with the bread crumbs mixed with cheese and put into heat-proof dish. Pour boiling water around them, about 1 inch deep. Put dish in 350° F. oven and heat until rest of dinner is ready. Heat for at least ½ hour.

Cucumber Mousse   (Serves 4 to 6)

1 package lime gelatin
1 cup hot water
½ cup Chablis, or any white wine
1 teaspoon lemon juice

Green food coloring
1 cup thick cream, whipped
2 cucumbers, peeled and diced
1 avocado, peeled and diced

In the morning, dissolve gelatin in hot water. Stir in wine, lemon juice and couple drops green food coloring. (You want it pale green, not Christmas green.) Fold in whipped cream, cucumbers and avocado. Pour into individual molds and chill until dinnertime.

To serve, unmold on dinner plates on a leaf of lettuce. Sprinkle with bit of paprika. As you are eating by the fireplace it's best to keep everything on one plate.

Port Parfait

Vanilla ice cream   Port*

In nice long-stem glasses—champagne or something equally festive— put scoops of vanilla ice cream. Top with ruby-red port. Serve glass on a dessert plate with a thin cookie.

* Buena Vista, Port (California)

Late Supper III   (Serves 6)

BAKED AVOCADO WITH CRAB MEAT
BLUE CHEESE ASPIC
TOASTED ENGLISH MUFFINS
CRÈME LOIRE
COFFEE

WINE TO SERVE:

Almadén, Green Hungarian (California) or
Chevalier-Montrachet (French) or
Gallo, Rhine Garten (California)

Baked Avocado with Crab   (Serves 6)

1 can white sauce
1 teaspoon salt
½ teaspoon pepper
1 teaspoon Worcestershire

1 tablespoon sherry
1 large can crab meat (6-ounce
    or larger)
3 avocados
½ cup grated sharp cheese

Melt sauce in pan and add the seasonings and sherry. Drain crab meat and add. Heat. Peel and split the avocados in half. Fill with the creamed crab. Sprinkle with the cheese and put into heat-proof dish. Pour in ½ inch hot water and bake for 15 minutes at 350° F.

Blue Cheese Aspic   (Serves 6)

1¼ cups tomato juice
⅛ teaspoon basil leaves, crushed
    (rub with fingers)
¼ teaspoon salt
1 package lemon Jello
¾ cup sauterne or any white
    wine

3 tablespoons vinegar
⅓ cup Roquefort cheese (1 me-
    dium pie-shaped wedge, crum-
    bled)
1 small carton sour cream
1 teaspoon horseradish

Heat the tomato juice, basil and salt to boiling. Add Jello and stir until dissolved. Remove from heat and add wine and vinegar. Chill until mixture begins to thickens. Stir in crumbled cheese.

Pour into individual molds and chill in refrigerator until dinner time. Do all this in the morning.

To serve, unmold on lettuce leaf on salad platter or plate, and top with dollop of sour cream mixed with horseradish. Arrange on platter if serving buffet.

Crème Loire

1 quart vanilla ice cream
2 boxes raspberries or boysenber-
ries, fresh or frozen

Triple Sec or Cointreau

Put scoop of ice cream in champagne glasses, one glass per dinner guest. Wash and hull berries. Put in blender for just a couple seconds. Spoon over ice cream and pour teaspoon of liqueur over each.

When He Says "Let's Go Back To Our House After the Ball Game"

The answer, of course, is a casserole. With each one serve a tossed green salad, toasted sourdough rolls, beer in icy mugs from the freezer —or a good wine—and you have the perfect menu for after any sporting event.

Shrimp Mini   (Serves 4 to 8)

¼ cup olive oil
1 clove garlic, crushed
2 pounds shrimp, shelled and cleaned
1 tablespoon Worcestershire sauce
3 dashes bitters

1 cup sherry
1 cup chili sauce
½ teaspoon salt
¼ teaspoon pepper
1 cup grated Cheddar or sharp cheese

Actually you can make this casserole in the morning and reheat. But it only takes about 45 minutes or so to cook and it smells so good I cook it in an electric frying pan on the coffee table in the living room while my guests have that first welcome beer and discuss the last touchdown. Just be sure to have all the ingredients ready in the refrigerator so you can assemble them the minute you hit the house.

Heat the oil in the fry pan and sauté the garlic for a couple of minutes. Add shrimp and cook until light brown. Add everything else but the cheese and simmer for about 45 minutes. Last, stir in the cheese just until it melts. Ladle over hot rice.

WINE TO SERVE:

Charles Krug, Traminer (California)
   or
Almadén, Grey Riesling (California)
   or
Paul Masson, Emerald Dry (California)

Lobster, Venice   (Serves 8)

2 tablespoons butter	1 bay leaf
1 medium onion, chopped	1 teaspoon salt
2 cloves garlic, crushed	¼ teaspoon pepper
1 cup tomato paste	1 cup white wine
¼ cup chopped parsley	¼ cup brandy
1 teaspoon thyme leaves	3 cups cooked lobster meat

Assemble your ingredients in the morning so you can make this after you arrive home. I have a tea cart that I find a wonderful aid to being organized. Put your spices, liquors and other nonperishables on the top shelf and the plates underneath. Take perishables out of the refrigerator just before serving, put on cart and wheel to wherever you are going to "perform."

In casserole over Sterno burner, or in electric fry pan, heat butter and sauté onion and garlic for 5 minutes. Remove from heat and stir in everything but lobster. Put back on fire and bring to boil. Reduce heat, simmer for 15 minutes, covered, and then add lobster and heat through. Serve over hot rice.

WINE TO SERVE:

Cresta Blanca, Pinot Chardonnay (California) or
Schloss Vollrads, Kabinett (German) or
Gallo, Chablis Blanc (California)

Super Crêpe Casserole   (Serves 12 extremely fortunate people)

This is quite a project, so don't attempt it at the last minute. Make in the morning and refrigerate. Don't panic. This isn't as hard as it sounds and it's well worth every effort. It's done in four steps.

STEP I: Boil 4 breasts of chicken. Cool, pick meat off bones and cut into bite-size pieces.

STEP II:

5 tablespoons flour	4 tablespoons butter
2¾ cups boiling water	¼ cup cream
1 cup grated Swiss cheese	

In saucepan blend flour with water, a little at a time. Add butter. Heat and stir until smooth. Add cream, blend, then add cheese. Keep heating, stirring until blended and smooth. Makes about 4 cups sauce.

STEP III:

2 packages frozen chopped spinach	2 tablespoons butter
	2 green onions, chopped with tops

Cheese sauce (made in Step II)

Cook the spinach according to directions. Drain. In small frying pan, melt butter, sauté the onions, add to spinach. Add ½ cup cheese sauce.

STEP IV:

1½ tablespoons butter	1 green onion, chopped
½ pound fresh mushrooms, sliced	2 8-ounce package cream cheese

Cheese sauce (made in Step II)

Melt butter in frying pan and sauté the mushrooms and onion. In saucepan, heat the remaining ½ cup cheese sauce and add the cream cheese. Heat until they are smooth. Add the mushrooms and onion.

The next operation is to make up a package of popover mix, using 3 eggs and 1¼ cup milk instead of whatever they tell you.

Heat 1 teaspoon butter in frying pan and make 14 thin *thin* crêpes. This you do by putting 1 full tablespoon of batter in pan, tipping pan so batter runs and covers, and then turning when bottom side is brown. Stack the crêpes on cloth towel as you make them.

Now take two casseroles and in one build the dish like this:

1 crêpe on the bottom

(and a crêpe placed between layers of each of the following:

Spinach mixture, mushroom mixture, cooked chicken, spinach mixture, mushroom mixture, cooked chicken and end with spinach mixture.

Remaining cheese sauce is poured over the top layer and topped with: 3 tablespoons Parmesan cheese mixed with 3 tablespoons butter.

Repeat this process with other casserole, only start with the mushroom mixture topping the first crêpe. Bake for 30 minutes at 350° F.

WINE TO SERVE:

Wente Brothers, Grey Riesling (California) or
Buena Vista, Green Hungarian (California)

Sunday After Whatever Brunch   (For up to 16)

WHOLE COLD POACHED SALMON WITH SPINACH MAYONNNAISE
TWO-TONE TOMATO ASPIC
TINY ROLLS
FRESH FRUIT

Note: The breakfast menus in Chapter I are also good for brunch. Take another look.

WINE TO SERVE:

(For brunch I start serving wine as soon as the guests arrive.)
Bertolli, Soave (Italian)
    or
Italian Swiss Colony, Chablis (California)
    or
Wente Brothers, Dry Semillon (California)

This Sunday brunch should be planned in the spring so you can use your garden. Cover the table in marine blue, serve the salmon on a large wooden platter and arrange the fresh fruit down the center of the table. Line wicker baskets with bright napkins and fill with the tiny rolls. Use flower pots of blooming spring bulbs for a centerpiece.

Whole Cold Poached Salmon   (Serves 8 to 16)

3 cups water	1 piece celery
1 pint white wine	Juice of 1 lemon
1 onion stuck with a couple of cloves	12 peppercorns
	1 tablespoon salt
1 teaspoon thyme	Several sprigs parsley

Whole salmon (9 to 10 pounds)

In a deep pan large enough to hold the whole fish, combine everything but the fish. Bring to a boil and simmer for 20 minutes. Place salmon on a triple-layer of cheese cloth, leaving ends long enough to use as handles when lifting the fish. Lower the fish into the liquid. It should be completely covered.

Bring to a boil, reduce the heat and simmer for 6 minutes to the pound. Gently lift out fish on cloth and allow to cool.

Just before serving, lift fish to wooden platter and slide out cheese-cloth. Remove the skin and slip out the backbone; it's not difficult. Arrange lemon slices down the middle of fish. Sprinkle with a little paprika and chopped parsley. Salmon is best served cool, but not cold.

Spinach Mayonnaise

1 box frozen chopped spinach	1 teaspoon tarragon leaves
1 tablespoon chopped parsley	2 cups mayonnaise
1 tablespoon chopped chives	1 teaspoon dry mustard

Salt to taste

Cook spinach just until thawed. Do not overcook. Mix rest of ingredients and add to spinach. Let stand at least two hours. Makes about 3 cups dressing.

If there is any salmon left over, make this mold the next day:

Salmon Sauterne Salad

1 envelope unflavored gelatin	Juice of 1 lemon
¼ cup cold water	¼ onion, chopped fine
1 cube chicken bouillon dissolved in 1 cup hot water	1 cucumber, chopped (optional)
½ cup California sauterne	Salt
	Pepper

Soften gelatin in ¼ cup cold water, then dissolve in the hot chicken bouillon. Add rest of ingredients and pour into well-oiled mold, fish-shaped if you have one. Chill and unmold on a bed of lettuce. Serve with mayonnaise.

Tomato Aspic   (2 rings of 2 layers each) (Serves 16)

LAYER I:

2 cups tomato juice	1 teaspoon salt
2 cups Snappy Tom Bloody Mary Mix or Mr. and Mrs. T.	2 avocados, peeled, cut into small pieces
2 packages lemon Jello	1 green pepper, chopped
1 cup chopped celery	4 green onions, chopped including tops
1 jar pimiento-stuffed olives, sliced	

Juice of 1 lemon

Heat the tomato juice and Bloody Mary mix together. Dissolve the Jello in it. Let cool and add other ingredients. Pour into two ring molds and chill until firm.

LAYER II:

2 packages lemon Jello
3 cups water

1 cup mayonnaise
2 large packages cream cheese

Dissolve Jello in hot water and chill until syrupy. Beat in mayonnaise and softened cream cheese. Pour over firm first layers. Chill until ready to unmold.

Nothing better for a snack than a truly great *"hot sandwich."*

Baked Tacos Sandwiches   (Serves 6)

½ cup olive oil
4 cloves garlic
2 large purple onions, chopped
1 can taco sauce (Ortega Brand)
Salsa
2 small cans tomato sauce

1 teaspoon sugar
Bacon fat or lard
12 corn tortillas
1 pound Tillamook cheese, sliced
2 medium-size avocados, peeled
  and sliced

Carton sour cream (8-ounce)

In a deep saucepan heat oil and garlic. Remove garlic when it's brown. Add onions and sauté until golden brown. Add taco sauce, Salsa, tomato sauce and sugar. Simmer for 45 minutes. This can be done in the morning and reheated.

Heat about ¼ inch fat in heavy skillet. Fry tortillas one at a time, first on one side and then the other, leaving them still quite flexible. Across the entire diameter of each tortilla, place a slice of Tillamook and slice of avocado.

Fold the tortilla in half, secure with a toothpick, and arrange in a baking dish. When all the tortillas are done, pour the sauce over all and bake in a moderate oven for 25 minutes.

Serve two to a customer, with a tablespoonful of sour cream on top.

TO SERVE:

Cerveza Mexicana or
André, Sparkling Burgundy (California) or
Buena Vista, Sparkling Sonoma (California)

Swiss Toast   (Serves 6)

12 slices white bread
¾ cup butter, softened
6 slices Swiss cheese

2 eggs
1 cup milk
1 teaspoon salt

Spread the bread with ½ cup soft butter and make 6 sandwiches. Beat eggs with milk and salt. Dip cheese sandwiches in egg mixture and sauté in ¼ cup butter until brown on each side.

Serve with hot blackberry syrup.

Foster's English-muffin Pizza   (Makes 8)

1 can pizza sauce
Mozzarella cheese

Anchovies
Stuffed olives, sliced
4 English muffins, split and toasted

Spoon pizza sauce over each muffin half. Top with cheese, anchovies and sliced olives. Put under broiler until cheese melts and bubbles.

If using as a snack, serve with sliced tomatoes, pickles and hot peppers. Great!

Cheese, Beer and Olive Rarebit on Corn Bread   (Serves 4)

2 tablespoons butter
1 pound aged American or Cheddar cheese, grated
1 egg
1 teaspoon dry mustard
½ teaspoon salt

½ cup beer, heated
1 tablespoon Worcestershire sauce
12 (or more) ripe olives, sliced
Corn bread (or toast)
Paprika

Make in double boiler or in chafing dish on coffee table in front of the fireplace. Put butter in chafing dish. Add grated cheese. Stir until cheese is melted. Add beaten egg, mustard and salt. Cook and stir constantly. Gradually pour in beer and Worchestershire sauce. Add olives. Continue stirring. Serve over cornbread or toast. Sprinkle with paprika.

When He Says . . . "Come Back for Dessert and Coffee"

A treasury of incredible edibles: Most truly elegant desserts deserve an occasion all by themselves. Few stomachs can handle a soufflé *after* a several-course dinner.

The Soufflé

Yes, it may fall—but you can burn toast, overcook a roast and singe vegetables. Yet it's easy to make a soufflé if you just follow a few simple rules.

The sauce must be of the consistency of thick white sauce. The egg whites should be whipped just to the point where they hold distinct, moist-looking peaks. You may be tempted to beat the whites to very stiff, shiny peaks, but don't.

One cup of sauce provides adequate support for four to nine eggs. Extra yolks give a soufflé greater stability. Additional whites make the texture airier.

Folding whites into sauce

1. Fold in half the whites thoroughly.
2. Fold in the other half but less thoroughly.

I find it better not to butter a main course soufflé dish. But for a sweet dessert soufflé, butter dish, then dust with sugar. For any soufflé to look its best fill dish ¾ full. If container is not ¾ full, mixture will not rise above the rim, and the top will not break attractively. If filled more than ⅔ full, make foil collar to support the soufflé and prevent its overflowing as it bakes. After the soufflé is partially set, gently slip off the collar so the sides will brown.

Before baking, draw a circle with the tip of a spoon. This will encourage soufflé to break attractively.

When the soufflé is done, it feels firm when lightly tapped and the cracks look fairly dry. You can safely leave a baked soufflé in the oven for 5 minutes without disaster. But naturally, it should be served as soon as possible.

To start a soufflé ahead of time, prepare the sauce, separate the eggs (butter the dish if for a dessert soufflé) and heat the oven to 375° F. To complete preparations, add yolks to sauce, whip whites and fold into sauce. Proceed as recipe directs.

Grand Marnier Soufflé   (Serves 6)

4 tablespoons butter
4 tablespoons flour
1 cup cream (half and half will do)
Dash salt
6 eggs, separated
¾ cup sugar

Grated peel of 1 orange
1 cup whipping cream, whipped
1 tablespoon Grand Marnier, to flavor cream
¼ cup Grand Marnier liqueur to flame

In a saucepan melt butter and blend in flour. Stir in cream and salt and cook until thick. Remove from heat. Beat in yolks, ½ cup of sugar, orange peel and ¼ cup Grand Marnier. Whip whites until they hold distinct peaks. Fold half the whites thoroughly into sauce, then gently fold in the remaining whites until barely mixed.

Pour into a buttered sugar-dusted 2-quart soufflé dish. Fit a lightly buttered foil collar around dish (it should extend about an inch above the rim). Bake in a moderately hot oven, 375° F., for 15 minutes, then remove collar, but do not remove soufflé from oven. Continue baking for 20 to 25 minutes.

Over each serving, spoon whipped cream flavored to taste with Grand Marnier. Warm a ladle of Grand Marnier, flame it, and dribble over the top after you cut and serve it. Yum-yum!

WINE TO SERVE:

Chateau Climens (French
or
Novitate, Angelica (California)

When He Says at 2-30 A.M.: "Come for A Champagne Breakfast"

Menu I

BAKED TOMATOES WITH RICOTTA CHEESE
SCRAMBLED EGGS
TOAST AND COFFEE

CHAMPAGNE TO SERVE:

Korbel, Brut (California)
  or
Eden Roc (California)

Refrigerate, serve cold, cold, cold! as soon as guests arrive.

Baked Tomatoes with Ricotta Cheese   (Serves 6)

6 firm tomatoes
Salt
1 pint ricotta cheese
¾ cup soft bread crumbs
1 clove garlic, crushed
1 teaspoon parsley

1 teaspoon chopped chives, fresh
  or frozen
½ teaspoon sugar
1 teaspoon basil
Pepper
½ cup grated sharp cheese

Paprika

Slice stem end off tomatoes and gently scoop out pulp to leave a thick shell. Reserve pulp. Sprinkle inside of tomatoes with salt and invert to drain on paper towel. Blend ricotta cheese, crumbs, garlic, parsley, chives, sugar, basil and pepper. Chop tomato pulp to make ½ cup. Add to cheese-crumb mixture and blend well.

Stuff tomatoes nearly full with this, top with grated cheese and dash of paprika. Put in refrigerator until ready to bake.

To bake, put in shallow pan, pour in ¼ cup boiling water and bake in 325° F. oven for ½ hour. Tomatoes should remain firm and filling should have the consistency of cottage cheese.

Menu II: Champagne

POACHED EGGS IN ARTICHOKE HEARTS
CHEESE AND MUSHROOM SAUCE
TOASTED ENGLISH MUFFINS

CHAMPAGNE TO SERVE: (Cold, cold, cold)

Taittinger, La Française, N.V., (French)
  or
Beaulieu, Champagne (California)

Artichoke Hearts (Serves 8)

Cut 8 artichokes in half across the middle. Scoop out prickly section in fleshy heart. Carefully peel away tough green leaves, leaving only enough of them to form a cup around the bottom or "heart." Boil hearts for 7 minutes in white wine. (Do this in the morning, but do not refrigerate.) Poach 8 eggs and with a slotted spoon carefully put one in each heart. Cover with this hot sauce when ready to serve:

Cheese Mushroom Sauce

2 cans cheese sauce   ½ pound sliced fresh mushrooms
¼ cup butter

In large skillet melt butter and sauté the mushrooms. Add cheese sauce and heat until smooth and heated through.

NOTE: For additional great breakfast menus, see Chapter I

What to Feature After Making Love

While he drifts off to dreamland, slip out to the kitchen and fix a platter of fresh fruit, cheese, cold meat or chicken, buttered bread or a few crackers. Grab a cold bottle of champagne, two chilled crystal glasses and repair to the bedroom.

What did Scheherazade know about it anyway . . . all those stories. . . .

 **XII**

When It's Just You Two

The real test of how much you truly care is what you do for him when you're completely alone. And that includes cooking. . . . If you act as if you're doing him a big favor to tie an apron around your middle and heat up a can of soup, you know what you'll get? A tomato-soup lover. But offer him one of these treats and who knows *what* he'll become in your life?

THE SENSUAL
SUNDAY BREAKFAST

On that certain Sunday morning when it's going to be just you two, serve breakfast in the sunniest corner of the bedroom.

Menu

LIQUID SUNSHINE
HONEY CAKES WITH STRAWBERRY SAUCE
THICK BACON, CRISP
HOT COFFEE
WARM KISSES

Liquid Sunshine   (Serves 2)

Frost champagne glasses in the refrigerator, rub rims with lemon slice, then dip rim into powdered sugar. Shake off excess. Put ½ teaspoon granulated sugar in each glass, a dash of bitters and a thin slice of orange. Fill to the top with champagne.

Honey Cakes

3 eggs
¾ cup creamed cottage cheese
1 tablespoon honey
¼ cup sifted flour
¼ teaspoon salt

Separate eggs. Beat whites until stiff but not dry. Beat yolks until thick and lemon-colored. A wire whisk is good for the egg yolks but not for the whites. Stir the cottage cheese and honey into the beaten yolks. Add flour and salt. Carefully fold this mixture into the beaten egg whites.

Drop by tablespoonful into hot, lightly greased iron skillet and fry on each side until golden brown. This makes about a dozen tiny pancakes.

Strawberry Sauce

1 10-ounce package frozen strawberries
½ cup water
Dash salt
3½ teaspoons cornstarch
2 teaspoons lemon juice
Red food coloring

Thaw strawberries and drain juice into a saucepan. Add water and bring to a boil. Add berries, dash of salt and cornstarch blended with small amount of water. Stir and cook until thickened. Add lemon juice and a couple of drops of red food coloring.

SATURDAY AFTERNOON
BREAD-BAKE

Pick a Saturday when he's planned to watch an especially good sporting event on TV. While he happily watches the game, make a big pot of heavy stew with wine gravy. As the stew simmers, bake (from scratch!) a loaf of crusty French bread. Oh, those sexy smells!

Menu

HEADY STEW
BUTTERED NOODLES
FRENCH BREAD
TOSSED GREEN SALAD
BROILED FRUIT
COFFEE

WINE TO SERVE:

Almadén, Gamay Beaujolais (California)
or
Christian Brothers, Pinot St. Georges (California)
or
Gallo, Paisano (California)
or
Paul Masson, Rubion (California)

Heady Stew

5 onions, peeled and sliced
2 tablespoons bacon drippings
3 pounds lean beef stew meat
cut in bite-size pieces
1½ tablespoons flour

1 teaspoon seasoned salt
Coarsely ground pepper
1 bouillon cube dissolved in ½
cup hot water
1¼ cup Burgundy

½ pound fresh mushrooms, sliced

In Dutch oven, sauté onions in bacon grease until brown. Remove. Brown meat on all sides, adding a bit more grease if necessary. When browned, sprinkle with flour and seasonings. Add bouillon and 1 cup wine and mix well. Simmer very, very slowly for 3¼ hours, adding more wine if necessary. Then put onions in along with mushrooms. Stir well and continue cooking for 1 hour longer.

Just before serving, add ¼ cup Burgundy. Serve over slices of hot bread, or shell of round loaf or French bread.

Homemade French Bread

1 package active dry yeast
1½ cups lukewarm water
½ cup milk
1 tablespoon butter

1 tablespoon sugar
1½ teaspoons salt
5 cups sifted bread flour
3 tablespoons milk

3 tablespoons sesame seeds

Soften yeast in ¼ cup of the warm water. Stir to dissolve and let stand for 5 minutes. Scald milk. Add butter, sugar and salt. Let cool. Pour into large bowl. Add yeast mixture and 1¼ cups water. Stir in flour, working it with hands. Knead until smooth and elastic. Cover. Let rise in warm place until doubled in bulk. Shape into 2 balls. Let rest for 15 minutes.

Shape each ball into a roll 15 inches long, tapered at each end in traditional French-bread-loaf shape. Place on baking sheet liberally sprinkled with cornmeal. Cover with towel and let rise until double in bulk (about two hours in a warm place).

Brush loaves with milk and sprinkle tops with sesame seed. Make several diagonal gashes ½ inch deep in top of each loaf.

Heat oven to 450° F. Place a large pan of hot water on lower shelf. Place baking sheet containing bread on upper shelf. Bake for 10 minutes. Reduce heat to moderate (350° F.) and bake for 50 to 60 minutes.

If you want to try something different, sometime bake one loaf in a round Pyrex casserole. When done, cut off the top crust, pull out the warm inside bread, and fill crust shell with the stew. Put the pulled pieces of bread on a cookie sheet, dribble melted butter over them and heat for a couple of minutes. Serve in a bread basket.

Broiled Fruit

Peel and quarter 2 pears and cut into thin slices lengthwise. Arrange about 1 cup fresh or canned pineapple chunks in layer over pears. Dot with about 2 tablespoons butter. Sprinkle with ⅓ cup brown sugar and 2 tablespoons cognac. Slip under broiler until fruits are heated through and sugar bubbles.

THE ART FILM

On a gloomy Sunday afternoon ask him to take you to an "adult" movie. (Sexy.) Come home, have dinner in front of the fire and maybe make love on the rug.

Menu

GIN MARTINIS WITH SINFULLY LARGE OLIVES
HEARTH-ROASTED POTATOES
ONE STEAK FOR TWO
SLICED TOMATOES
TIPSY POUND CAKE

WINE TO SERVE:

Château Margaux (French)
or
Gallo, Hearty Burgundy (California)
or
Inglenook, Cabernet Sauvignon (California)

Hearth-roasted Potatoes

In the morning wash two baking potatoes, rub with bacon grease and wrap securely in aluminum foil. When you come home from the movie light the fire in the fireplace. Put potatoes up next to the hot logs, but not in the flame. They should take from 30 minutes to an hour, depending upon the fire. Test by sticking with a long-handled barbecue fork.

One Steak for Two

Buy a good sized chunk of top sirloin (at least 2 pounds). Put into a glass pan and crush 3 cloves of garlic (in press) over the top. Pour on a good bottled marinade or 1 cup red wine and let sit out while you go to the movie.

When ready to serve, broil for about 15 to 20 minutes per side. Slice in thin diagonal slices.

Tipsy Pound Cake

Thin a jar of raspberry jam with port. Heat and pour over a slice of pound cake.

BATHTUB COCKTAIL PARTY

It's Saturday night and, grudgingly he has consented to go to the charity ball at the Country Club. He's had his tuxedo cleaned and pressed, found all his studs and even bought a new pair of patent leather shoes. What love!

When it's time to start thinking about getting dressed, suggest that the two of you have a cocktail in the bedroom while you shower and change. But instead, fill the tub with hot water, bubble bath and perfumed oil. Put the cocktails on the edge of the tub, untie his bathrobe and invite him to join you in the bubbles!

Music Under the Stars

On an especially balmy afternoon in late summer have cocktails on the patio and sip, holding hands, as the sun goes down. Then serve dinner right where you are sitting.

Menu

HIS FAVORITE COCKTAIL
STEAK LOUISE
MUSHROOMS VERMOUTH
SALAD MARIO
BRANDY BOATS
COFFEE

WINE TO SERVE:

Château Lafite-Rothschild (French)
or
Inglenook, Carbono (California)
or
Almadén or Louis Martini, Cabernet Sauvignon (California)

Steak Louise

This is my version of the Steak Diane served in especially fine restaurants.

2 tablespoons butter

2 pieces top sirloin put through
   meat tenderizer

1 clove garlic

Seasoned salt

Seasoned pepper

1 teaspoon dry mustard

1 tablespoon Worcestershire

A-1 steak sauce

In iron skillet, melt butter until hot and bubbly. Drop in steak and fry quickly. Mash clove of garlic over meat. Add salt and pepper. Sprinkle on mustard and turn steak. Quickly add Worcestershire and enough A-1 sauce to cover bottom of pan. Remove meat to plate and bring sauce to boil. Pour sauce over meat. Serve with Mushrooms Vermouth.

Mushrooms Vermouth

2 tablespoons butter

½ pound fresh mushrooms

1 tablespoon dry vermouth

Pinch rosemary

Melt butter in pan. Add mushrooms, vermouth and rosemary. Gently sauté until mushrooms are brown. Do the mushrooms before the steak and keep warm on back of stove.

Salad Mario

1 tomato, chopped

1 green pepper, chopped

2 green onions, including tops,
   chopped

½ cucumber, chopped

Mix together and add tart French dressing. Do your chopping ahead of time and add dressing just before you start steak. You want everything to come out even and on time.

Brandy Boats

2 oranges

Vanilla ice cream

Brandy

Cut through the rind around middle of oranges. Plunge into boiling water and let stand for 5 minutes. Remove oranges and cool slightly. Carefully pull half of the rind up to form a cup on the top of each orange; pull the other half down to form a base. Do this in the morning and store in refrigerator.

To serve, put a scoop of vanilla ice cream into each cup. Press a sugar cube into top of ice cream. Heat brandy in ladle and then ignite. Pour, flaming, over the ice cream. Be generous. Whatever brandy is left in the orange you drink. Yum! and the orange can be eaten, too.

A HAPPY MEMORY

Surprise him by re-creating the exquisite late-afternoon lunch the two of you shared on the veranda of say, the Queen's Park Hotel in Jamaica that time you slipped away for a week you couldn't really afford.

Luncheon in Jamaica

BURGUNDY COOLER

LAMB SALADE

HOT FINGER ROLLS

CHEESE AND FRUIT

Burgundy Cooler

1 ounce peach brandy
1 ounce curaçao
½ small bottle of soda water

1 small bottle Burgundy
Sugar
2 pieces of fruit (peach half, pear half or whatever)

Mix all ingredients except fruit with ice cubes in a chilled pitcher and stir until cold. Add sugar if you like. Pour into champagne glasses over pieces of fresh fruit.

Lamb Salade

2 cups diced cold roast lamb
2 cups diced cold cooked potatoes
1 cup French dressing
6 stuffed olives, chopped

3 green onions, including tops, chopped
2 teaspoons capers, drained
1 tablespoon shredded mint leaves

Seasoned salt, pepper

Mix everything and serve in individual lettuce-lined wooden bowls.

HIS FAVORITE RESTAURANT DISH

Every man has a favorite dish that he always orders at his favorite restaurant. Call the chef and ask him for the recipe. (P.S. If the chef is uncooperative, your local food editor on your local paper can probably get it for you.)

My all-time-favorite man's favorite dish (besides me) happens to be:

Linguini alla Vongole   (Linguini with clams)

1 pound linguini
¼ cup olive oil
2 cloves garlic, chopped
2 shallots, chopped
½ teaspoon pepper

1 teaspoon oregano
1 teaspoon chopped parsley
½ cup dry white wine
½ cup clam juice
2 dozen clams, rinsed

1 tomato, chopped

Cook linguini in boiling salted water for about 8 minutes. Drain, but do not rinse. While linguini is cooking, make sauce. Heat oil in skillet, add garlic and shallots and cook until lightly browned. Add pepper, oregano, parsley, wine, clam juice, clams and tomato. Cover and cook for about 5 minutes over high heat. Clams open when cooked. Do not overcook clams or they will toughen. Mix cooked linguini into clam sauce. Serve at once.

TO SERVE:

Soave Bolla (Italian)

or

Robert Mondavi, Pinot Chardonnay (California)

or

Charles Krug, Chenin Blanc (California)

XIII

A Word About Wine

by FORDEN ATHEARN

There is much romance, tradition and folklore about the making, selection, tasting and use of wines. There is also much nonsense. This wine mystique has given rise to a good deal of the nonsense and snobbishness, with the result that the housewife is frequently frightened off.

The Wine Snob

One kind of snob makes a great fetish out of selecting *the* correct wine for *the* certain dish, allowing for no other. This is nonsense. You should drink whatever wine you like with the food you are serving. Traditionally, however, red wines are considered to best complement heavy meats, beef, lamb and venison; white wines to complement fish, fowl, veal, eggs and soufflé dishes. Light red wines are traditionally considered best to complement starches—rice, spaghetti, noodles and all types of delicious Italian paste dishes (or as the Italian says *pasta*) like linguini, taglierini, vermicelli, fettucini, cannelloni. And don't forget the Mexican dishes. A light red wine goes well with tamales, enchiladas and tacos.

Another kind of snob is the import snob: "If it's imported, it must be better." It is not my purpose to disparage another country's wines. I have enjoyed delicious French, Italian and German wines both at home and abroad. I've also drunk some terrible European wines, and so have you. Of course you can get some European wines in this country (at high prices) that are out of this world. But don't count on them. Frankly, imported table wines tend to have oxidized slightly and be *too* old.

Also, some wines don't travel well. Yes, this is true. Wine is a living liquid and subject to change in the bottle. The brother of the fine Italian bottle you enjoyed in Bologna or Florence may taste quite differently when you encounter him in Chicago. European wines are also more subject to vintage change—good and bad years—depending upon the weather. The same vineyard that one year produced an outstanding wine may produce a mediocre one the next year.

On the other hand, our American wines, particularly the California ones, are more consistent in quality because the climate where they are grown is more consistent. For example, the San Francisco fog that drifts into the Sonoma, Napa and San Joaquin valleys helps to provide an even temperature and keeps the vines from freezing in the winter and from getting too hot in the summer. In short, the beginning wine host or hostess would be well advised to stick to California wines. As a result of these conditions they are more apt to be consistently good.

As to the comparison of European and California grapes themselves, most California grapes are from European cuttings. And most of the European and California vines are grafted to native American rootstocks. Amazing, but true. In the 1860's a tremendous blight (phylloxera) swept over most of the French vineyards. To control the insect, the French vintners imported phylloxera-resistant rootstocks from the U.S. Therefore it can be said with some accuracy that American vines saved the French wine industry.

Next, and closely akin to the "import" snob, is the price snob: "If it's expensive, it's got to be good." This is obvious nonsense. When a great vintage becomes rare, this causes a rise in price. Often, however, this rare vintage ceases to be worth the high price. It can be too old, have oxidized, or become murky. I don't wish to imply that the least expensive are necessarily the best, but by no means always are the most expensive absolutely the best.

One final word about the reasonably priced California wines: The great vintners who make them have a reputation of growing and buying fine grapes. Their wines are produced in great quantity without any diminution of quality. California State law imposes the strictest quality regulations of all its governmental agencies. It does not permit the addition of sugars or other sweeteners. The quality is in the wine. The taste is a matter of individual preference.

The last type of snob is the genuine expert. Wine is his hobby. Simply by tasting and without looking at the bottle, he can tell you whether a wine is foreign or domestic, what region it is from, what type it is, what vineyard it comes from, what year it is and even on which side of the hill the grapes were grown. You may enjoy his expertise, but don't let his superior knowledge cow you or keep you from drinking and enjoying what *you* like.

The Various Kinds of Wines

RED WINE: It is not the purpose of this chapter to present an encyclopedia of wines or even a definitive treatise on wines. We simply offer a short description of the types of wines most readily available in this country.

Table wines are those we drink with meals. They may be red, pink or white; dry or sweet; light or heavy.

The most common red table wine is Burgundy. Pinot Noir, Gamay, and Red Pinot, called varietals, are Burgundies, named after the variety of grapes from which they are produced. Burgundy is dry, robust and traditionally fuller bodied than other red wines. Pinot Noir is soft and velvety with a fine bouquet. Gamay is a little lighter in body and color than Pinot Noir.

Claret is another red table wine. It is dry, tart and lighter-bodied than Burgundy. Cabernet, Zinfandel and Grignolino are claret varietals, named for the grapes from which they are produced. Cabernet differs from most clarets because it is fuller bodied, deeper in color and has a more commanding bouquet.

Bordeaux is a red wine from the Bordeaux region of France. It is generally less full-bodied than a French Burgundy.

Chianti is a dry, slightly tart, full-bodied wine, traditionally Italian and served with *pasta*.

Rosé is a pink wine, fruity, light-bodied and fairly dry.

WHITE WINE: White table wines may be divided into three groups: Sauterne, Rhine wine and Chablis.

Sauterne is gold in color, full-bodied, fragrant and may range from dry to sweet. It's varietals are Semillon and Sauvignon Blanc. Semillon can be dry or sweet. Sauvignon Blanc is usually dry. Haut Sauterne is usually sweet with a delightfully rich aroma and is popular as a dessert wine.

Rhine wine is dry, tart, light-bodied with a flowery bouquet. It is pale green-gold in color. It's varietals are Riesling, Traminer and Sylvaner. Riesling is delicate in flavor. It is frequently identified further by the grapes from which it is made, such as Johannesberg Riesling. Traminer is a spicy and fresh-tasting Rhine wine.

Chablis is dry and fuller bodied than Rhine wine. Pinot Blanc, Pinot Chardonnay and White Pinot are the best-known varietals of Chablis, again, named for the grape varieties from which they are made.

APERITIF OR BEFORE-DINNER WINE: Sherry, vermouth, Compari and Dubonnet are wines to serve before dinner instead of the traditional cocktail. The true gourmet would rather sip an aperitif than dull his palate and senses with hard liquor.

Sherry is rich, has a nutlike flavor and ranges from dry to sweet. Pale golden to dark in color. The sweet or cream sherry is more a dessert wine than other sherries.

Vermouth is spicy, aromatic and has an herb flavor. Its two most common varieties are dry and sweet. The dry is light straw color; the sweet is darker and reddish in color.

Compari, an Italian aperitif, is similar to Dubonnet, but with a somewhat bitter flavor.

Dubonnet, a French aperitif, is heavy and sweet, red or white in color.

Vermouth, Compari and Dubonnet, red or blond, go well with soda and are enhanced by a twist of lemon peel.

DESSERT WINES: Port, Tokay, muscatel, Angelica and cream sherry are dessert wines.

Ports are rich, sweet, fruity and fairly full-bodied. They are generally deep red to pale gold or tawny.

Tokay is a pinkish amber color with a slightly nutty or sherry-like flavor. It is less sweet than port.

Muscatel is sweet, fruity and full bodied, dark amber or red in color.

Angelica is amber-colored, very sweet and resembles white port.

CHAMPAGNE: Champagne is, of course, sparkling; generally white, sometimes pink. Very dry is *brut*, the semi-dry is *sec* and the sweet is *doux*. Champagne has no rules. By the very serving, it makes any occasion festive, any meal a feast. It can be served for breakfast, brunch or luncheon, with hors d'oeuvres before dinner, along with the entrée or as a companion to dessert.

Serving of Wines

The wineglass is placed to the right of the water goblet. The bottle should be put on the table near at hand. The wine is usually passed or served as soon as the first course or entrée has begun.

In opening the wine bottle, first cut the bank or cellulose with a sharp knife. This will keep the bottle neat-looking. Wipe the bottle mouth before inserting the corkscrew, and again after the cork is pulled. A good corkscrew makes wine serving very simple, so have a good one. Many vintners have abandoned the cork altogether and use a screw cap which eliminates the need for a corkscrew.

Uncapping a champagne bottle is different. You simply twist, loosen and remove the wire hood. The foil comes off with it. Hold your thumb on the cork so it won't pop out. Slant the bottle away from the guests, twist the cork gently, or work it from side to side. Hold on to it as it leaves the bottle. (It will still pop.) You should have a glass handy to catch the first foam.

Customarily, the host pours a little wine into his own glass first, to taste it and be sure it is good. Also, it gives him and not his guests any bits of cork that may be near the top of the bottle.

Never fill a wineglass more than one-half to two-thirds full. The air space above the wine gathers an aroma and bouquet which is essential to the enjoyment of the wine. (It also lessens the chance for spilling.)

After pouring wine, give the bottle a slight twist before raising it from the glass. This catches the last drops from the bottle's lip and avoids dripping.

If you wish to be fancy, you can put unchilled wine in a basket or cradle. This is not necessary unless you have a very old red wine and wish to avoid stirring up any sediment that may be in the bottle.

You might want to use an ice bucket to chill wine. Most people, however, prefer to chill wine in a refrigerator. But if you do use a bucket, keep it handy to the dinner table and dry the bottle with your napkin before pouring.

It is generally considered poor form to wrap a wine bottle in a napkin, thus hiding the label. The custom of wrapping the bottle originated with restaurateurs who didn't want to show their patrons what wine they were serving.

If you purchase wine in bulk—a cask, gallon bottles or jugs—you may transfer a portion to a decanter with a funnel. Cut-glass decanters or glass liter bottles are decorative but not an essential part of serving wine. If you are going to leave wine in a decanter, be sure it has a tight stopper. This, however, is not a good practice with slightly sweet table wines. If any yeast reaches the wine, it will ferment.

The large bottle of dinner wine (fifth size) will pour six servings, averaging about four ounces each. Dessert and appetizer wines are usually poured in smaller servings, two and one-half to four ounces.

Wine may be served in any glass, even a tumbler, but a stem glass adds to the beauty of your table and to the enjoyment of the wine. Also, a stem keeps your hand from warming the wine.

If you want to find out the correct wine glasses to use for the various wines and the occasions on which to use them, write for a free illustrated booklet showing them and giving descriptions. The address is: Miss Marjorie Lumm, P.O. Box 732, Sausalito, California 94965. Miss Lumm is the Director of the Wine Institute Home Advisory Service. To learn more about the uses and the full enjoyment of wines, write to: Wine Institute, 717 Market Street, San Francisco, California 94103. They will send you a free home study course, published by the Wine Advisory Board of the California Department of Agriculture, a non-technical and easy-to-follow schooling in wine uses.

Care of Wine

Dinner wines, because of their alcohol content, are perishable once exposed to air. Once opened, they should be used within a few days, kept recorked and recapped in the refrigerator. Gallon bottles, after opening, may be decanted or transferred to smaller bottles which have been sterilized by boiling. Fill, leaving about an inch from the top (to allow for expansion) and recork, or use a screw-cap bottle. Save dinner wine left from the meal and use later in cooking.

Open red wines about an hour before you intend to serve them for the flavor really comes up when the wine is allowed to "breathe." Serve and keep red wine at a cool room temperature. In very hot weather you might want to chill a red wine for a while. This is a matter of personal taste. However, once a wine has been chilled, do not store it again at room temperature. White and rosé dinner wines are generally chilled in the refrigerator one to three hours before serving.

Champagne should be chilled for 2 to 4 hours in the freezer (or at least 6 hours in the refrigerator); use immediately after opening, before the sparkle is lost. Returned to the refrigerator, it will be good for a couple of days, but it won't have the same bubbliness, although sometimes a few bubbles will appear the next day. Use leftover champagne for cooking—it's especially delicious for chicken.

Because of their higher alcoholic content (about 20 percent) dessert and appetizer wines will keep up to several months after being opened. Keep them at cool temperatures, with a good cork or stopper.

Store unopened wine in a cool, dry place where the temperature will remain fairly even. Ideal storage temperature is between 50 and 60 degrees; 70 degrees is considered the highest safe temperature for long-term storage. Never chill a wine below 35 degrees. Avoid extreme changes in temperature. Don't store wine near furnaces, water heaters, steam pipes or radiators, and keep wine out of sunlight.

Bottles containing corked wines should rest on their sides so they will stay airtight and so the corks will remain moist. If you leave corked wines in their case, turn the case on its side. Screw-cap bottles may stand upright.

If you have a wine cellar or closet, store the sparkling and white dinner wines in the lowest rack or bin because it is cooler there. Store the red wines in the next section up. Dessert and appetizer wines may be stored on top, because they are the least affected by higher temperatures.

If sediment appears in wine, stand the bottle upright for one or two hours before serving. This sediment is harmless and will settle on the bottom. But avoid shaking the bottle. Pour the wine gently, or decant it into another container.

Cooking With Wine

Not wishing to infringe upon the domain of the author—this is after all a cookbook—it must still be said that, in our humble opinion, nothing adds to the flavor of a good dish, sauce or soup like wine. Nothing tenderizes a meat like wine. You can take a tough old piece of beef and marinate it in red wine for 4 to 6 hours and it will become as tender as a mother's heart.

We think you can add wine to any dish and it will be improved. Try white wines and champagnes for cooking fowl, fish, chicken and veal and a red wine for red meats. But this is not our department. The recipes herein are liberally laced with wine. The author agrees that most cooks don't use nearly enough wine. And you can serve the entire family as the wine loses its alcoholic content in cooking. The alcohol passes off at about 172 degrees, well before the boiling point. Only the subtle wine flavor is left. Incidentally, along with the alcohol, most of the calories disappear.

Recommendations

With each menu for which a wine would be appropriate, we have recommended wines which range from the rare and costly to the more available and reasonably priced.

We did not wish to rely upon our own judgment exclusively, so we've called upon the knowledge, palates and experience of three gentlemen whom we have been privileged to know both as friends and connoisseurs.

Judge Marcel Biscay is a wine authority as well as a gourmet. When he is not dispensing justice in our California courts, he vacations in the wine districts of his ancestral France. He visits the wineries and the families that produce the wines, partaking also of the gourmet dishes which they complement. After carefully reading the manuscript, he has made a true connoisseur's recommendations.

Dr. Benjamin Ichinose has undoubtedly one of the finest private wine cellars in America. He collects vintage wines as an art patron collects old masters. He and his wife, Mayon, spend days in the preparation of the food that is served at their table. After a dinner party in their home, each guest is presented with a copy of the menu, including the names of the wines served with each course. Both Dr. and Mrs. Ichinose spent a great deal of time going over this manuscript, selecting the wines they felt best accompanied each menu.

The name Gallo is undoubtedly well known to you. Ernest Gallo's modesty would forbid his saying it; his company is, nevertheless, the largest vintner in the world. In addition, he is one of the most sensitive gourmets we've ever known. His wife, Amelia, is a culinary genius who takes the time to produce those delicate dishes you read about but seldom taste. Ernest Gallo has read this manuscript and recommended many of the wines.

For my part, as an attorney I am in no way connected with the wine industry. As a bachelor, necessity forced me to cook when entertaining at home. My knowledge of food and wine is self-taught. That's why I know what is confusing, what is simple. Much of what I have learned has been as Balli of the Hillsborough, California, Chapter of the Confrerie de la Chaine des Rotisseurs, the oldest Gourmet Society in the world.

To illustrate the power of good wines and gourmet cooking and the influence they can have on the male of the species, when this cookbook goes to press I will no longer be a bachelor. I will be married to the author of this grand book. What greater recommendation could I give!

CHEERS!

Hillsborough, California

ACKNOWLEDGMENTS

Every cook depends heavily on her friends to share their favorite recipes. Here's a list of my special friends who were, indeed, generous in sharing:

Mrs. Herbert Adair
Mrs. Robert Altic
Mrs. Thomas
 Armstrong
Mr. Otis Booth
Mrs. Roswell Burroughs
Mrs. Otis Chandler
Mrs. Hayden Clement
Mr. and Mrs.
 James Craig
Mrs. Skip Crist
Mrs. Howard Culver
Mrs. Vincent De
 Domenico
Mrs. John Elliott
Mrs. Alfred Ducato
Mrs. Lennart Erickson
Mrs. Harry Fain

Miss Frances Forden
Mrs. Dominic Fronteri
Mrs. Joseph Gleason
Mrs. Hugo Grenzback
Mr. and Mrs.
 Abe Ginnes
Mr. Paul Hazelrig
Mrs. Dorothy Heidt
Mrs. Ben Hoberman
Mr. and Mrs.
 Robert Hodes
Mrs. Sylvester Johnson,
 Jr.
Mrs. Ronald Klein
Mr. and Mrs.
 John Knowlton
Mrs. Edward Martin
Mrs. Pamela Mason

Mr. and Mrs.
 Donald Montague
Mr. Richard Ney
Mrs. Rudolph Pabst
Mrs. William Pochelon
Mrs. Harry Rinker
Mrs. Virginia Savage
Mrs. Norman Scheiber
Mrs. Bud Smith
Mrs. Owen Spann
Mr. and Mrs.
 Douglas Tuck
Mr. and Mrs.
 Allen Vejar
Mr. and Mrs.
 Robert Willis
Mrs. James Wood

Index to Recipes